MODEL MAGIC

Model Magic

by

Vic Smeed

in association with Ulster Television PLC

ARGUS BOOKS LIMITED

Argus Books Ltd.
1 Golden Square
London W1R 3AB

ISBN 0 85242 872 3

Phototypesetting by Photocomp Ltd., Birmingham

Printed and bound by William Clowes (Beccles) Ltd., Suffolk

Contents

Foreword

For children, toys are magic. For all of us, the art and skill of model-making – as the television series and this book show – is an illuminating learning experience.

MODEL MAGIC is a new series of six programmes produced by Ulster Television for transmission on Channel Four. The introductory programme deals with models and history and is followed, in turn, by programmes on cars and trams, ships and yachts, aircraft, railways, and finally miniature engineering.

The topics, techniques and problems of miniaturisation and working to scale are presented by Bob Symes, himself a model railway enthusiast, who interviews several model-makers with significant reputations in the field.

The purpose of this book is to support and develop viewer interest in the television programmes. It gives context to the individual model-making enterprises featured and we hope that it will have a life of its own, after the programmes have been seen, as an added stimulus for modelling activities.

What the programmes and the book attempt to do together is to open up the magical world of imagination, construction and appreciation of fascinating working models – a world constituted by excellence in planning and design, and extraordinary precision in scale and craftwork. Taken together, therefore, series and book may be considered as two of three main constituents in a truly educative resource pack: the third element, which makes the resource work, is your interest and enthusiasm for what you have seen and read and the extent to which you translate that into activity and initiative.

GEORGE FLEETON
Senior Education Officer
Ulster Television
September 1985

Introducing Modelling 1

It has taken many years for the public at large to accept that there is rather more to modelling than simply "playing with toys", which was the usual expression among the ignorant. The popular press and even, regrettably, specialist "full-size" publications loved to seize on an interest in models as indicating crankiness or mental immaturity, yet the evidence to the contrary has been plain for anyone who wished to see. Would many of the great yacht designers of the last 100 or more years and virtually all the major aircraft designers of this century have been model enthusiasts if models were no more than toys?

Models actually go back several thousand years, since models of ships and boats have been found in early Chaldean, Egyptian and other tombs. These were mostly clay or wood and no doubt had symbolic or religious significance. Votive ship models, made and hung in churches as an expression of thanks for deliverance from some nautical catastrophe, date back over 1,000 years and there are records of working models in Elizabethan times, including an all-metal hull!

Sailing models of ships would clearly have been the earliest form of working models since nothing else was capable of self-propulsion until the development of the steam engine, and even then the application of steam as a motive force was initially considered only for ships. As a source of power in stationary engines steam has, of course, a longer history and it is known that models were not only helpful in the evolution of large engines but that tools evolved for the construction of the models were enlarged and adapted to produce parts for the full-size engines. The wheel has turned and many of the fascinating early engines are now faithfully reproduced as scale working models by keen model engineers.

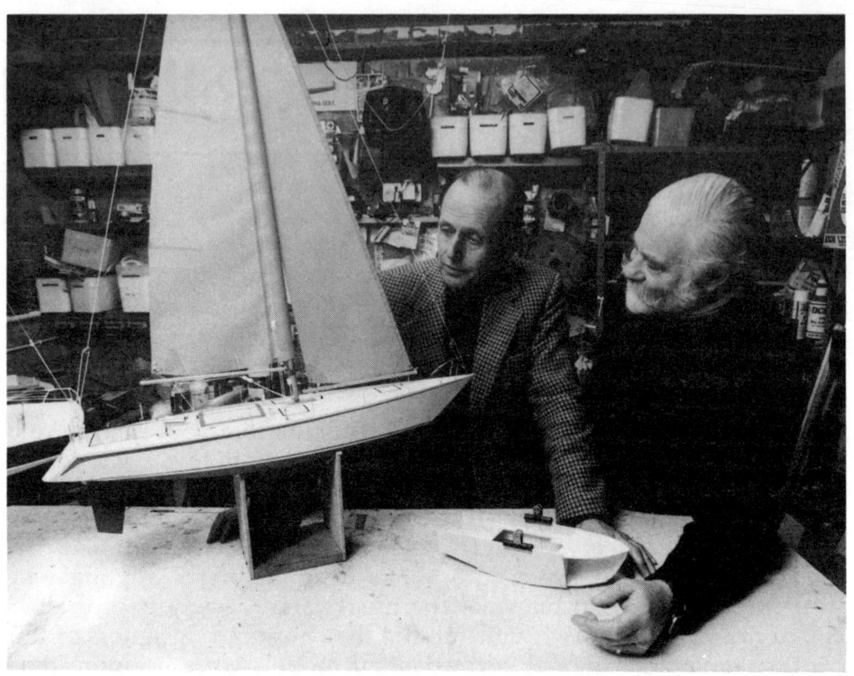

The author and Bob Symes, presenter of the Ulster TV *Model Magic* series,
discuss one of the former's yacht designs in Roger Stollery's workshop. On the bench
is the *Ulsterman* model, which appears later in this book, in its early stages.

Model steam engines for boat use could be bought in the 18th
century, towards the end of which the famous Round Pond in
Kensington Gardens, London, was constructed for the operation of
both sailing and power models. Only a little later the first successful,
repeatable heavier-than-air flights were being made, again by models,
designed and built by Sir George Cayley. In 1848 Henson and
Stringfellow's steam-powered model flew, and in the 1870s Frenchman
Alphonse Penaud was flying a variety of rubber-powered models.

Other flight pioneers – Lilienthal, Langley, A. V. Roe, Tom Sopwith,
the Wright brothers themselves and many other famous names – built
and learned from models, while on the marine side such giants as
Herreshoff, Nicholson and Stephens built and sailed models and
maintained a continuing interest in developments in model yachts.
The self-steering vane gear, much publicised at the time of Francis
Chichester's first solo round-the-world voyage, can be traced back in
models to 1875 (a design was published in *Model Engineer* in 1905) and

was in extensive use from the mid-30s onwards; Chichester in fact spent a lot of time at a model yacht club when evolving his version.

Static scale models have been used for centuries in ship-building, from simple half-models carved either to "prove" lines or to produce a shape from which sections could be scaled up, to the elaborately beautiful ship models which were produced in the 17th and 18th centuries when new designs were submitted to the Board of Admiralty; fortunately many of the latter survive so that our knowledge of the development of ship design and construction over the last 300 or so years is very detailed.

In the 19th century scientists such as Froude developed the practice of research by means of accurate measurement and observation of towed models, leading to the extensive use of models in test tanks and wind tunnels which is an essential part of any large-scale research and development today. This has been taken further by the use of "models" of large tankers and bulk carriers and the like which are built 20 or 30m in length and are used as small, practical commercial cargo vessels as well as providing data for the intended full-scale vessel which is built probably ten times the size. Scale

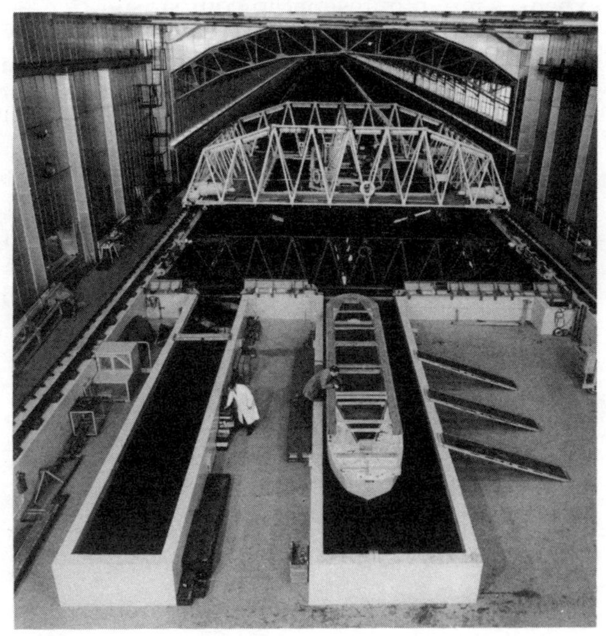

The size of test tank models can be seen as one is prepared for a towing test in No. 3 tank at the National Maritime Institute, Feltham. (Photo courtesy National Maritime Institute.)

tankers and warships are also built in sizes capable of accommodating a two-man crew, used for instruction in ship handling.

Unmanned aircraft models, often radio controlled, are used to establish the best procedures for ditching and to investigate unusual flight characteristics such as deep stalling and spinning. Accidents can be prevented, or at least hazards minimised, and thus lives saved, by such work with models, nor does it end there, for models can be used to investigate why or how a crash took place. Invaluable aid was provided in the explanation of the Comet airliner disasters by constructing models separating into fragments similar to the recovered parts of the full-size aircraft, catapulting the models and repeatedly blowing them apart until the pieces fell into patterns matching those of the actual crashes. Height, speed, attitude, sequence of break-up and many other parameters were positively established.

Radio-controlled aircraft have been used for more than 50 years as targets for ground-to-air gunnery and are currently beginning to expand in more peaceful pursuits such as aerial photography, flood observation and other activities where photographs, film or direct video transmission from an elevated viewpoint are of value. The initial cost of a camera-equipped radio model is a fraction of that of a manned aircraft or helicopter and its operation and maintenance expenses are infinitesimal in comparison.

Commercial use of models is, generally, in quite a different category from the widespread and more frequently seen hobby aspect; few modellers could afford the cost of what to a major manufacturer is a

This A-frame twin-pusher rubber-powered model is typical of model aircraft from about 1908 to 1930, though this example was built recently by one of the many present-day vintage enthusiasts.

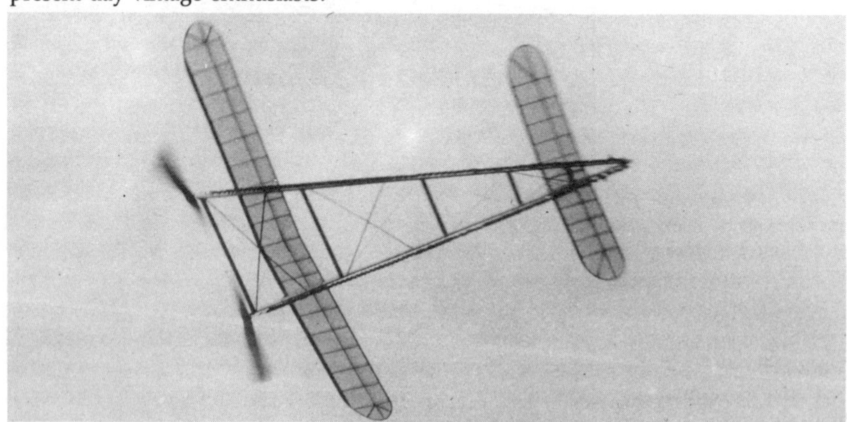

relatively inexpensive line of research. There is, however, a degree of overlapping. One water authority uses a radio aircraft to inspect its reservoirs and feeders; the model was designed and built and is operated by an employee who is also a keen and accomplished modeller. Again, for the America's Cup challenge, several model designers were each asked to design a 1/10 scale 12m yacht and these models were built and sailed against each other, with models of existing full-size designs, in evaluation trials which threw up a number of potential lines of exploration. One of the modellers later joined the design team working on the next challenge.

Schools

In many countries modelling is recognised as a valuable component in school curricula. It has been suggested that playing darts improves mental arithmetic in a pleasurable way, and this is doubtless true, but building and operating models offers this and a great deal more. Familiarity with tools and materials, development of manual dexterity and patience, reading plans and learning to plan step-by-step progress, awareness of physical laws and mechanics, recognition of cause and effect, stimulation of the mind and the acquisition of all sorts of nuggets of knowledge – including even self-awareness – are just some of the advantages which result when an interest in models is kindled. That these things are acquired unconsciously while indulging in an absorbing pursuit in no way lessens their value, and it is a lucky school which employs a teacher able to instil modelling enthusiasm in its pupils.

Informed estimates suggest that in Britain at least 1 in 25 of the population has made a working model at some time, that 1 in 100 will make occasional models and that probably 1 in 250 will maintain a lifelong and active interest. The total sales of specialist magazines on modelling subjects comfortably exceed half a million each month and there must be well over 25,000 modellers sufficiently committed to belong to a model club. This does not include the scores of thousands who assemble non-working plastic kits; these latter vary from the youngsters who glue the parts together without painting them (but who learn in the process) to those enthusiasts who create miniature masterpieces, painstakingly researched and often modified to specific machines which, if cleverly photographed, are indistinguishable from photographs of the prototypes.

There is something of a pattern in working model activity. Many schoolboys and some schoolgirls are interested at an early age, most frequently in aircraft, which are relatively quickly built and require no elaborate tools or facilities, or, in the 1980s, in radio-controlled cars, which are usually in kit form and need little in the way of tools to assemble. Some show a keen interest in power boats or yachts. There are, of course, vast numbers interested in model railways or slot-racing cars, but, initially at least, these do not involve much actual construction of the models. Relatively few participate in model engineering unless an adult encourages them, although there are always examples of projects by talented youngsters at exhibitions.

By the time they are students as opposed to schoolchildren the numbers have thinned a little but the particular model area is taken more seriously. A more scientific and/or experimental approach is often taken, or efforts are made to improve performance, either model or personal. These are the people who will return to modelling from time to time in later life.

Return? Yes, because marriage and the establishment of a home and family often tend to take priority in the 20 – early 30 age group. Some model activity may continue but usually on a reduced scale. Return to fuller activity occurs when home, family and career are settled, sometimes because the old enthusiasm has never been lost, sometimes because the growing family is old enough to participate, and sometimes simply because financial commitments now allow a little more expenditure on hobbies. There have also been many instances where a father has only started to build models at this stage, as a worthwhile pastime to interest and encourage his sons, and become an enthusiast himself.

With maturity comes the willingness to spend longer on actually building a model, leading to scale model radio aircraft, yachts, scale ships, hand-built electric locomotives and rolling stock and the like. Some can at last afford a lathe and other tools to make live steam models; model engineering tends to appeal to a slightly older average age-group whose members have acquired the skills and facilities needed and who may well have more time to undertake long-term projects. Three or four years to build a 200 lb passenger-hauling steam locomotive is considered quite quick!

Generalisations such as these indicate only an overall pattern which, since modellers are strong individualists, must have many exceptions. Ambitions and abilities vary considerably, and it is quite possible to find a superbly built, advanced model which is the work of a newcomer to modelling standing next to a slightly rough, unreliable model which is the latest product of someone who has been modelling for years. One can admire the one for obvious natural ability and the other for persistence despite an obvious lack of

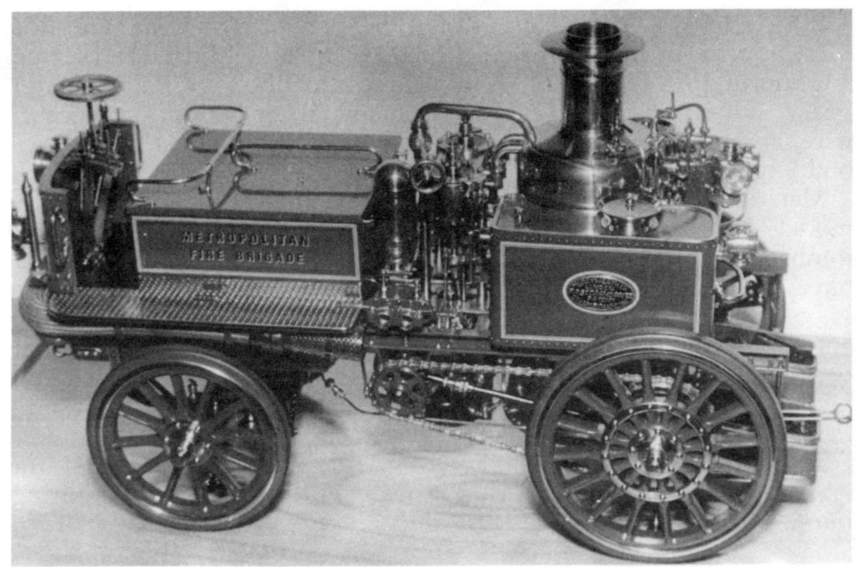

Model engineering at its superb best. This working Merryweather firepump was built by Miss Cherry Hinds (now Mrs. Hill) and is about 9in. long.
Nuts the size of pin-heads are split-pinned through!

aptitude. In model engineering in particular one frequently sees a butcher or an accountant producing work which can more than hold its own against that of a clubmate who is a fitter or turner by occupation.

Why build models?

Why people make models is a difficult question to answer. There can be a competitive element – to make a model aeroplane and trim it to fly is a challenge. To make it fly well, or to fly better than other people's models, simply extends the challenge. A model yachtsman may well want his boat to sail faster than others, but on the other hand he may be quite satisfied to see it pottering along on its own. To have created something from raw materials and to prove its correctness by watching it function is all the satisfaction he needs. An aeromodeller whose model flies out of sight and is lost views the event with mixed emotions – regret at the loss is mixed with pride and excitement that the model was efficient enough to take advantage of thermal currents and be borne away by them. Pride of achievement is undoubtedly a major factor in the pleasure of modelling, and this pride appears in various forms: actually completing the model, seeing it perform properly, and winning a competition are three major peaks, but cutting a piece of wood or metal, or bending a piece of wire, and finding it an exact fit is the sort of minor boost that makes building enjoyable.

Man has always been fascinated by miniatures and has made models for centuries. The clay ships and chariots in the Pharoahs' tombs may have been notional transport to the hereafter or they may have been favourite playthings or possessions. People with no knowledge of, or interest in, models like to own miniatures, as the enormous interest in Fabergé's creations demonstrates. In the Far East inter-village races with sailing models of local craft have gone on for centuries; much the same used to happen in the fishing communities of Britain and there are still some traces of the practice.

There remains the possibility of Man's subconscious thirst for knowledge. We have all no doubt heard that Man has an enquiring mind, but we do not necessarily recognise it in ourselves. To read

Featured in the television series is Alex MacFadyen with his incredibly detailed model of H.M.S. *Vanguard* which has won major awards at the Model Engineer Exhibition and other model shows.

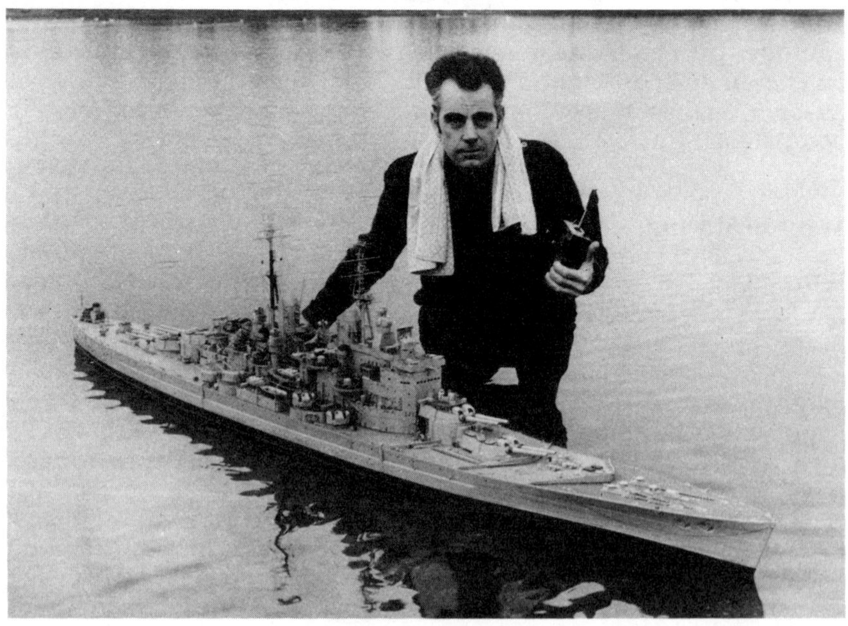

about something is not really enough, and there is no doubt that a model can teach. Even watching two sticks "race" down a stream reveals quite a lot about the stream's currents and eddies, endways and sideways resistance, the effect of water absorption and so on. A model opens the way to the exploration of the air, or the water, or of the expansive effects of steam or whatever. A baby explores textures and tastes but gradually grows accustomed to its known environment; is it not possible that the curiosity and need for personal experience remain, and in many individuals find an outlet in building and operating models?

How to start

Perhaps the most most remarkable thing about modelling is the enormous variety of subjects and approaches which are possible. This book, and the television series with which it is associated, give some idea of this choice. Every branch of the hobby divides into perhaps three main streams, and each of these sub-divides. The sub-divisions are further separated into specialised areas, and each of the following chapters sets out the relevant chain.

What is general is the simple fact that you can spend as much or as little on your chosen pursuit as you wish. Inevitably there are some people who will not feel satisfied unless they buy the biggest or latest, or best, in the belief that spending a lot of money will lead to success. At the other extreme are those who will derive their satisfaction by producing successful models in the cheapest possible way, from scrap materials or inexpensive everyday objects. As an example, one of the author's designs was for a 36 in. Restricted class yacht with a hull built mainly from empty cereal packets and mast etc. from a scrapped television aerial. Many examples of the design were built and it proved entirely competitive at national level; the only things that really had to be bought were sails, or sail material, adhesive and paint, as everything else could be "scrounged" by anyone prepared to do a little hunting.

A common remark by laymen is "It's an expensive hobby" and it can be. It is easily possible to spend £500 on an aircraft kit, engine and radio control equipment, but it is also possible to build and fly a radio-controlled model for about a tenth of this. Most of the cost will be the radio equipment, which will last for a number of models over several years. On the other hand, equal pleasure can be had from, say, a free-flight sailplane, which could be built for a couple of pounds and would involve no running expenses.

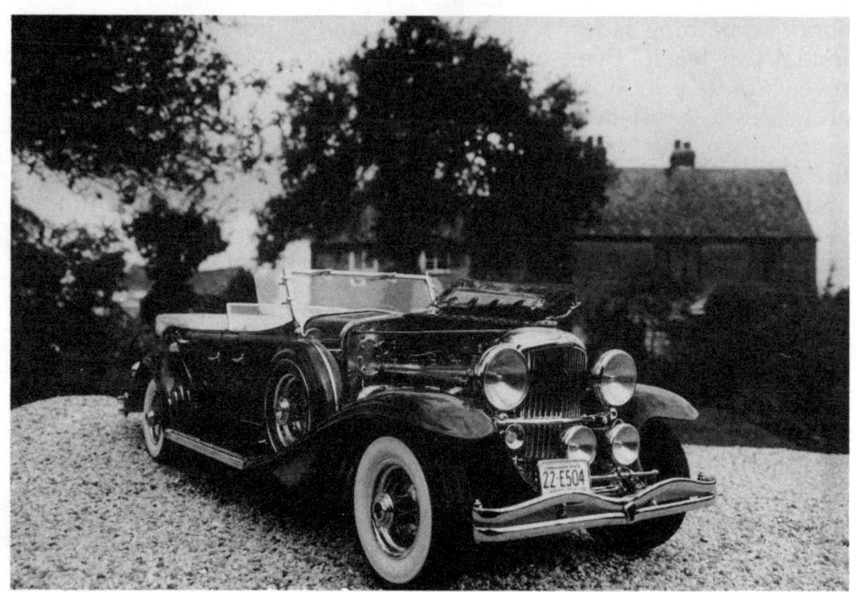

Static models can record the appearance of past machines. This splendid ⅟₁₅ scale Model J Duesenberg Derham Tourster might be the real car, so accurate and polished is the work of Gerald Wingrove.

To take another example, many spirit-fired small steam plants have been constructed from material picked up for a few pence at a scrapyard, without even the use of machine tools. A hand-drill clamped to the bench, or sometimes a basic electric drill, has been used to lap the piston to an adequate fit and virtually every other operation is then hand drilling, sawing, filing and soldering. Naturally a lathe makes things easier and widens the projects that can be undertaken, but all-metal engineering-type models can be built without one and with no great financial outlay. Where higher stresses and pressures are likely it is prudent to use the specified material rather than scrap metal, for safety's sake; the materials and castings for, say, a 5 in. gauge locomotive may seem expensive at perhaps a total of £200, but the expenditure is spread over a period and the job may take two or three years or more, so weekly average expenditure is not unreasonable. The finished model, if soundly built, will be worth a couple of thousand pounds and will last for thirty or forty years at least.

Most newcomers will know the general area which attracts them and the first step should be to find out as much as possible about the

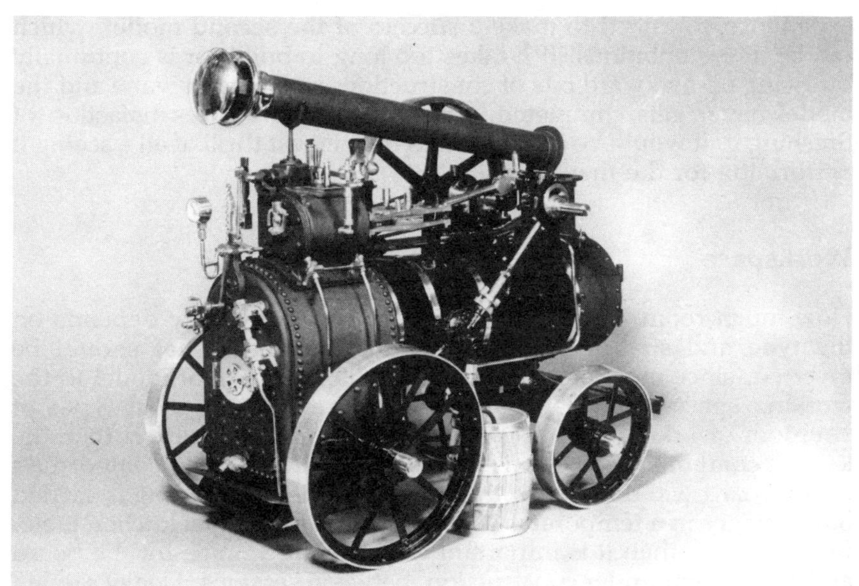

Research is usually needed to produce faithful replicas such as this Marshall portable engine, which preserves in three dimensions and minute detail a record of a steam application no longer in use.

subject. This means reading up-to-date magazines and books – the local library will obtain books for you – and asking about local activity at the nearest model shop. If there is a club the library should have details, or if a blank is drawn a stamped self-addressed envelope to the appropriate model magazine should give you a lead to follow.

You may not wish to join a club, but it is still worth getting in touch and going along to a meeting. Modellers are a friendly bunch and will answer questions or give advice if it is clear that you are genuinely interested. You may have seen a club in operation and if you wander over to the site and ask a question or two (provided that a competition is not in progress) you will pick up a good deal of useful information which should help bring your ambitions into focus.

The commonest mistakes beginners make are to undertake something too complex at the outset, or possibly something too small. A beginners' model should be simple and straightforward (which usually means that it is relatively inexpensive) and of moderate size. In general, the larger the model the easier it is to operate and, because the parts are less fiddly, the easier and quicker it is to build. It may not look exactly the way you would really like, but it will provide the experience you need to make a success of the second model, which can be more ambitious. If it takes too long to build, or is continually throwing up awkward bits of construction, interest can wane and the model never gets completed. Apart from losing the satisfaction of finishing it, it would be a pity to miss the biggest thrill of all – seeing it performing for the first time.

Workspace

How much room, or what facilities are needed, clearly depends on the type and size of model undertaken; perhaps that should be inverted, since most modellers would tailor the size of model to the working space available! The main requirement for most types of "outdoor" working models is a building board a little longer than the longest component to be constructed, but the width and composition of the board will differ with the type of model. If building is carried out in stages in a temporary workplace – the proverbial kitchen table, for example – then it is important to have safe storage for the board and component under construction, between sessions. Heavy sawing and shaping should be carried out elsewhere, in the garage or on the garden path etc. to reduce the noise and mess indoors. The same applies to painting and similar work, where possible, since the smells of some modelling materials may not be conducive to domestic harmony.

Small models, e.g. H0 locomotives or Peanut scale aircraft, need a board little larger than a pastry board and the quantities of adhesives, paints, dopes etc. are sufficiently small for nuisance to be minimised. Newspaper between board and table and a sheet of polythene spread on the floor beneath the working area will reduce the chances of scratching or soiling and often make it easier to find small components inadvertently dropped.

A permanent workplace is obviously much to be preferred, and this may be a bench at the end of the garage, a garden shed or, if you are lucky, a room in the house. In the first two instances temperature variation may be a problem, leading to condensation and rusty tools. If an electricity supply is available (desirable for lighting, soldering, power tools and so on) a small tubular heater is not expensive to buy or run: it won't really warm the workshop but it will keep the tools sufficiently off the chill to prevent condensation. Hand tools could be replaced in a box and kept indoors, but this is not practical with, say, a power fretsaw or a pillar drill.

Actual space required depends on the type of model and the extent

18

of the workshop equipment. An aeromodeller can work with a relatively light bench, a small vice and a few hand tools, but a model engineer will need a really solid bench and space for lathe, drill, grinder, storage cabinets and much else. An area of perhaps 8 x 6 ft. (say 2.5 x 1.8m) is just about a minimum in such a case, though an aircraft or boat modeller could probably cope in 6 x 5 or 7 x 5 ft., provided he stored finished models elsewhere. The model engineer needs a much more solid structure, especially the floor, which should be concrete, with a damp-proof membrane, to provide a firm base for the machinery. There are specialist books on workshop basics which go into the subject in great detail.

For working in wood one of the most useful acquisitions is a pair of old but firm stools, perhaps bought from a jumble sale. These, with two lengths of thick timber, can form a sawing bench or will accept the building board and allow all-round access, a particularly useful point when making a boat hull or even a large fuselage. Work on locomotives or petrol engines and the like requires a clean, flat and

Filming radio-controlled Marblehead class yachts at the Guildford club water took place in steady sleet. Fortunately yachts are made to sail in all weathers. Marbleheads, 50 in. long, are the popular class.

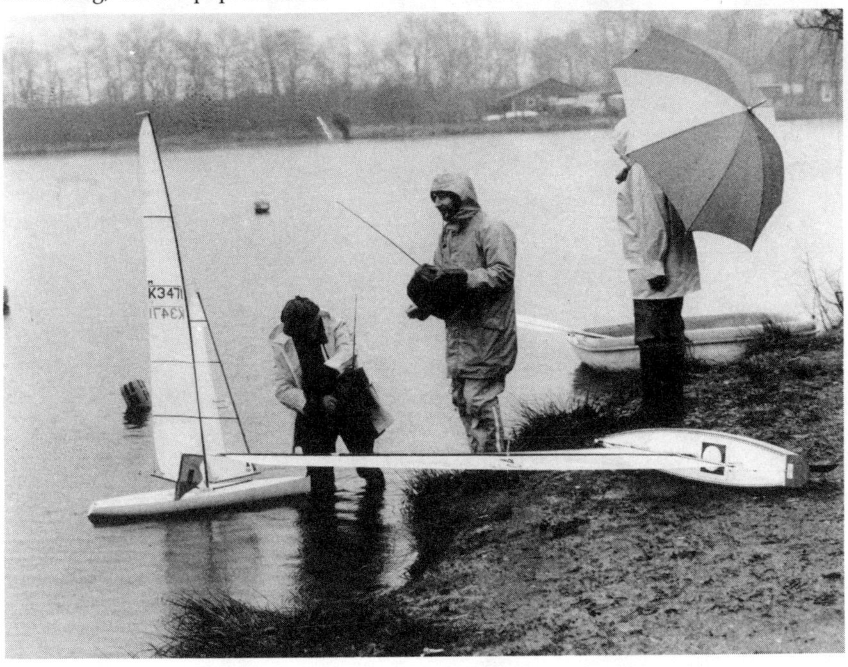

hard surface and a jumble sale or junk shop may yield the marble top of an old washstand, which is ideal when set on its own bench or on top of a chest of drawers. An alternative is a sheet of plate glass, which can also be used as a reasonable surface plate for marking out.

Devotees of modelling have one common characteristic, the magpie instinct. They collect books, magazines, drawings, materials and bits and pieces that may come in handy, and there is a general reluctance to dispose of models which are not currently in use. Storage space can thus be a problem, though the house loft often provides an answer for items required only rarely. Tobacco tins and similar can be used for screws, nuts and other small parts, a wipe of white undercoat on the top end allowing the contents to be pencilled on so that when the tins are stacked on a shelf identification is easy. Racks or boxes under the bench can be used for materials, or storage may be possible on a shelf or frame just above head height in a garage or shed.

Although space for construction is rarely a problem, a model railway layout requires permanent space. This is the 'Beverly' line, built by David Lowery and photographed by Brian Monaghan; it is seen in the television series,

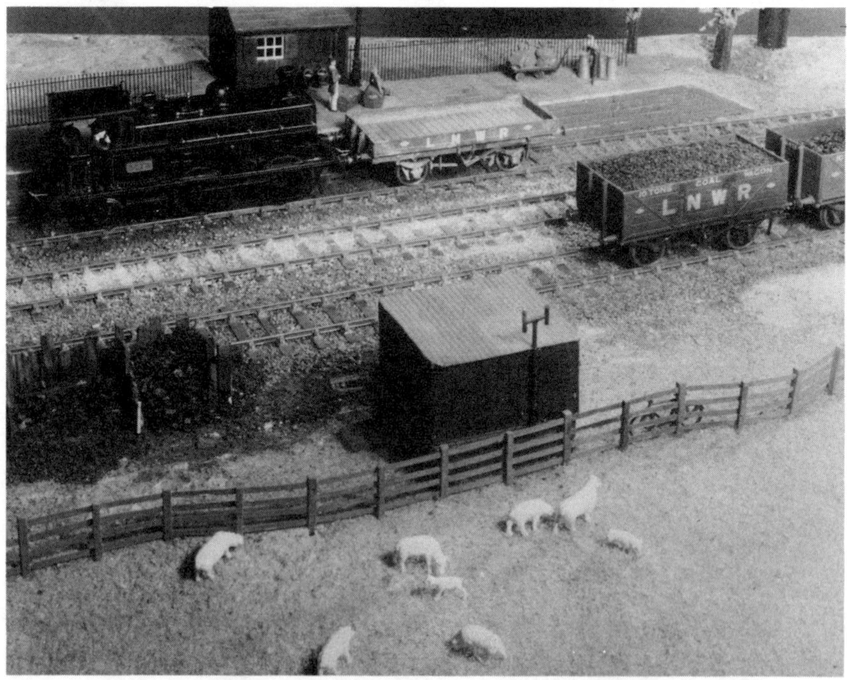

Tools

What type of modelling is pursued often dictates the tools needed, but another influence is the type of person concerned. Some can produce excellent work with the simplest of tools while others need a complete power workshop to hang a picture.

What can be said is that though poor work can be turned out with good tools, it is extremely difficult to produce good work with poor tools. Not impossible, note, but it does take much more time, effort, skill and experience. Good quality tools kept in good condition make work easier, quicker, more accurate and safer. You are less likely to cut yourself with a sharp chisel than a blunt one because you have more control and need less force. A screwdriver kept correctly ground and not used for opening tins is less likely to slip and damage the work or you, and so on. Time spent in tool cleaning, sharpening and lubrication will be saved over and over in work; watch a skilled craftsman at work and see how often he touches up the edges of his tools and how easy it then becomes to get a good result.

Some potential model-makers are deterred by the apparent outlay required for even a collection of hand tools. The answer is to buy the tools as the need for them becomes apparent, when a collection will be built up comparatively painlessly. Starting with a simple model normally means using only simple basic tools. The possible exception to this is in model engineering, where the need for machine tools is likely to be obvious from the outset. There are, however, many evening classes providing the use of all the tools one could possibly need, or there are scores of clubs with well-equipped workshops. Hand work and marking out the next steps are usually enough to keep one occupied between weekly or twice weekly visits and not only are the tools available but instruction and help are at hand. In addition, a newcomer is in a position to hear of good second-hand buys which could establish his workshop for a comparatively modest outlay and he is likely to be able to buy raw materials at remarkably low prices.

Clubs

There are hundreds of model clubs in the U.K., some of which may consist of only half a dozen members while others run to a couple of hundred or more. Most clubs are affiliated to one or more of the national governing bodies, part of whose function is to arrange national competitions, to maintain common rules and to administer

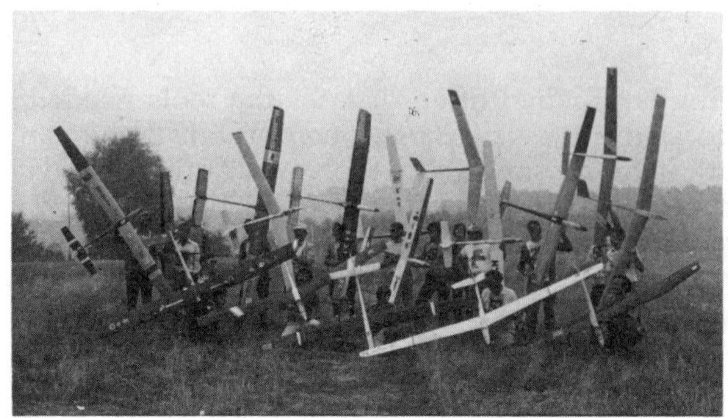

A cheerful band
of radio glider
enthusiasts pose for
for a photo for the
club album. Notice
the size of the
models, which
average between
100 and 120ins. span
for thermal, or flat
field, flying.

the particular branch of modelling in general. These bodies are usually divided into geographic areas and there are area competitions, while the clubs themselves frequently run competitions for members, or inter-club events etc.

A high proportion of members, many of long standing, have never entered a competition, or at most have only joined in a fun event at the club. Others may be keen competitors and spend every week-end travelling to some event or other. Model clubs are not like, say, tennis clubs, where applicants have to "play themselves in". On the contrary, complete beginners are welcome and there is always someone to advise and help. A beginner will learn more from half a dozen club meetings than he is likely to discover in two or three years of trial and error on his own, and it would be strange indeed if he did not enjoy the company of other enthusiasts.

Club fees are usually quite modest and often include insurance cover in the remote but possible event of a model causing damage or injury. Such cover is required by local authorities, the Ministry of Defence and other public bodies on whose ground models are operated. Some clubs offer "country membership" for people living too far off for frequent attendance and this is often well worth looking into by lone hands who may have no nearby club. Junior membership is usually available to youngsters sufficiently interested and some associations run junior competitions.

Like most worthwhile activities, club membership conforms to the adage "The more you put in, the more you get out". Join a club, join in the activities, give a hand if it's needed and not only will your modelling ability and enjoyment advance by leaps and bounds but a whole new dimension could be added to your life.

The horseless carriage made its debut just a century ago, and it is a fairly safe bet that someone was making models soon after. In fact, steam-powered wheeled vehicles go back further, 200 years in the case of William Murdoch's tricycle, and there are reliable records of a 17th century self-propelled carriage. However, there are few traces of enthusiast-built models between 1885 and the late 1920s, most of the replicas surviving from that period being tinplate toys, mostly from Germany, some of them very beautiful but not coming into the category of amateur built models. Some models were described in *Model Engineer* (1898 onward) but it was clearly a minority form of modelling, probably because of the difficulties of wheels and tyres.

"Formal" clockwork car racing, with hand-built models performing speed dashes, began at Cambridge in 1928 and spread to London in the 1930s, when rubber strip power began to vie with clockwork. There were some experiments with electric-powered cars, including racing them on a partitioned track. Several of the full-size motoring magazines gave space to these activities.

Small petrol engines, intended for aircraft use, appeared in the 1930s but models using them were banned in the 1939-45 war. Cars using these engines and running tethered to a central pylon made their debut in 1942 and "cable racing" was born. This form of running, with speeds of over 100 m.p.h., enjoyed five or six years of popularity after the war but died off after the introduction of factory-made American models which could equal or better home-built cars. Those able to afford to obtain one of these cars could usually win and this took much of the enjoyment away.

Another form of car racing, rail racing, had meanwhile arrived and lent itself admirably to the small compression-ignition engines ("diesels") produced in vast numbers in the post-war years. A large

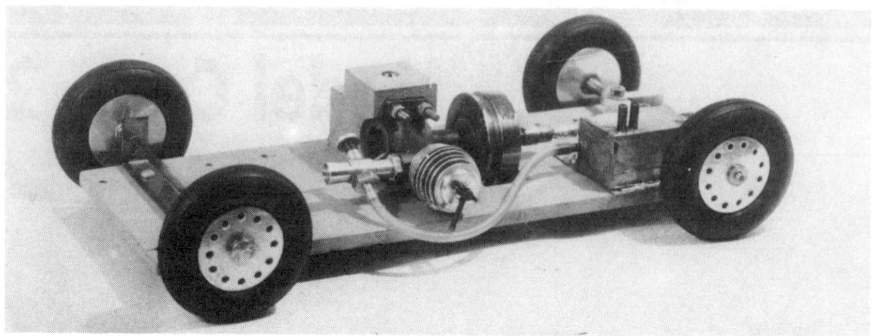

The simplicity of a diesel rail racer, ca. 1952, is clear in this picture. An air-cooled
·75cc diesel drives the rear wheels by bevel gears and there is no steering.
Zonkers are beneath chassis plate.

track consisted of four tubular rails secured on spacers, to which the
cars were clipped by zonkers, which were vertical ball-raced bobbins
in pairs holding the cars securely to the rails. Clutches were fitted so
that simultaneous stationary starts could be made, and some of the
more sophisticated tracks had a power-driven roller in the track
surface at the start position. Speeds were not all that high, but the
cars looked fast and exciting and they were of course racing against
each other rather than a stopwatch.

This form of racing petered out in the early 1950s, partly because of
the cost of building a track but also due to clubs not being prepared to
enter into litigation with a company which claimed patent rights on
the form of zonker in use. As it happened, electric rail racing was

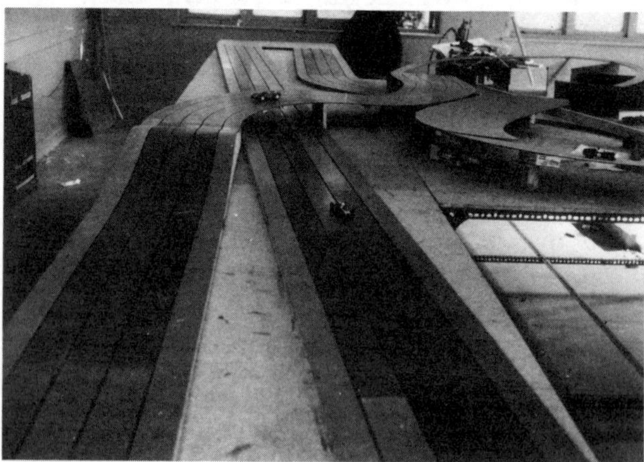

The Clarendon
Circuit under
construction by the
author and Alec
Gee. This track was
the scene of the
first-ever National
Championship for
electric slot cars,
in 1964.

introduced at this time; the cars were much smaller (1/32nd scale) and had the considerable advantage of variable power input controlled by the owner. In other words, they were driven by the owner and driving skill became as important as construction and preparation, a much more attractive proposition.

Various experiments had been made during the 1930s and '40s with electric cars run on a track of some sort, but the overall conception of several cars guided by rails and with controllable power was a new and instantly successful combination. The presence of rails projecting above the track was generally acceptable, but the idea of a slot for guidance in lieu of a rail appealed more to some enthusiasts as giving free sliding and possibly requiring more skill in driving, as well as being less visually obtrusive. Eventually simple methods of track manufacture were devised and, after some years of rail versus slot controversy, the last rail track was converted in 1964.

Thousands of modellers enjoyed this new form of car racing and there was strong commercial support, from small accessories to complete sets of track, cars and controllers et al. The best racing was on the large, hand-built club tracks and car performance developed swiftly in the competitive atmosphere. Much the same pattern was followed by groups of enthusiasts in other countries until the idea of pay-tracks, with if required hired cars, was conceived in the U.S.A. Large commercial tracks sprang into existence all over the country and with them came the funds and pressure to develop ever-higher performance.

Pay-tracks did not meet the same response in Britain, but the increasingly powerful, and expensive, motors were imported. The cost of building a competitive car soared and its competitive life was shortened to the extent that many average club members gave up. The pay-track craze disappeared as quickly as it had appeared but by then slot-racing in Britain had been reduced to about a tenth of its support plus one or two manufacturers producing sets for, basically, the toy market.

Radio Control

Car modelling entered another quiet period as far as working models were concerned. There were always the relatively small number of builders making static models and the die-cast collectors' market continued to expand. Cable racing re-emerged in two or three European centres, on a small scale, and there were scattered experiments with radio controlled models, which had been known since

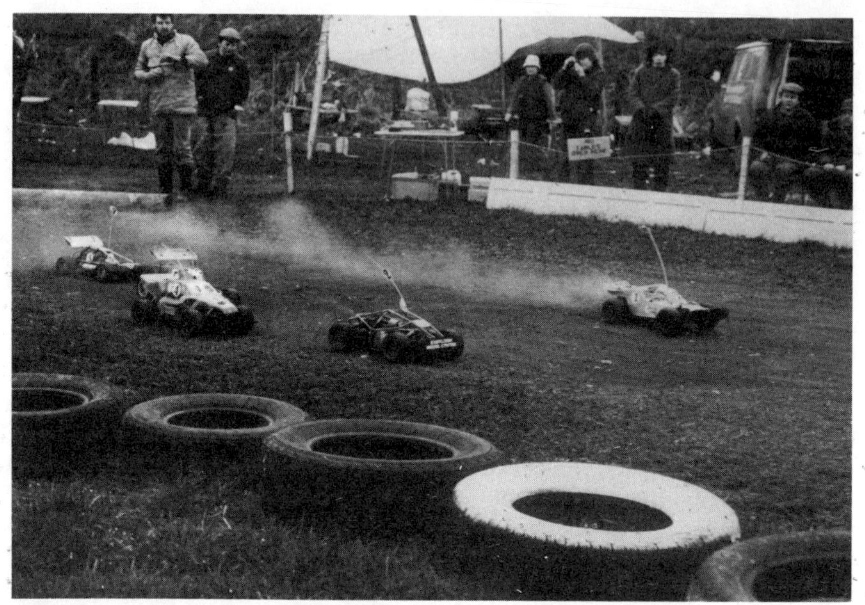

One-eighth scale ic-engined buggies racing. Glowplug engines are used, with a maximum capacity of ·21 cu. in. (3·5 cc), and the drivers have full control over steering, engine throttle, and even braking.

1948. One of the recurring major problems for the average modeller has been the availability of wheels and tyres and, for working models, the difficulty or expense of drive mechanisms.

All this was to change in the 1970s when English and Japanese firms introduced kits for radio-controlled cars, but the change was not overnight. In fact it took six or seven years for this "new" branch of model cars to become really popular with average modellers, by which time the early enthusiasts had developed the models to a point where a solid foundation for the sport had been evolved. There are those who feel that circuit-racing cars peaked in 1982/3 and that enthusiasm has now lessened, but on the other hand there has been an enormous growth of interest in off-road vehicles or "buggies", which are now the most popular area. One obvious advantage is that buggies can be run virtually anywhere, without the need for a special track or surface.

The broad classifications are internal combustion, electric, and buggies, which can be i.c. or electric. All 'use similar radio, giving steering and speed control plus, often, braking, and electric models usually have the capability of reversing. In all cases electric cars are to

26

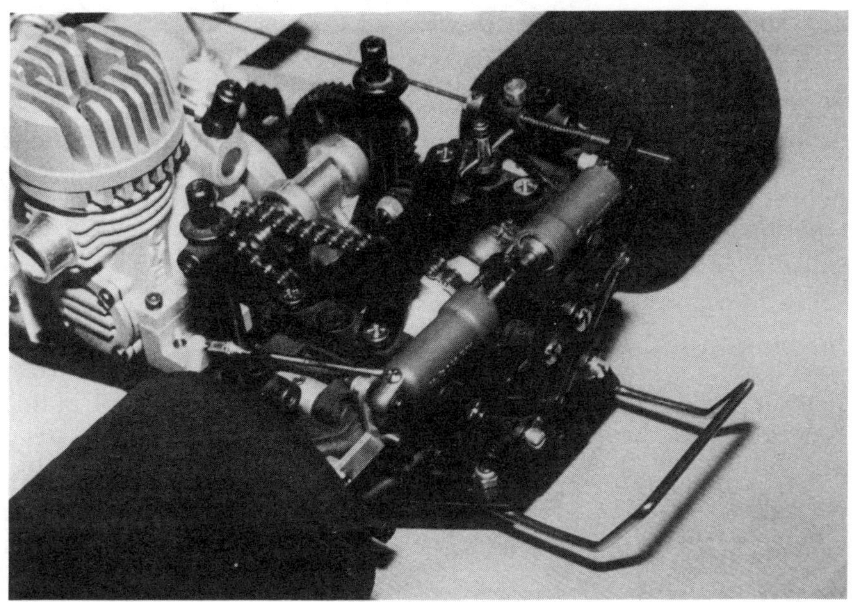

Chain is used for the final drive on this ⅛th scale car. Note the suspension dampers (the two horizontal cylinders) and general sophistication. The rod by the offside-wheel is the brake rod; the brakes are discs.

a nominal 1/10 scale and i.c. engined cars to ⅛; there are some 1/10 i.c. engined models but these are rarely seen in Europe.

Electric cars are most frequently raced indoors, in ballrooms and sports halls and the like, using tracks delineated by scooter tyres and adhesive tape or some such non-permanent marking. Glow engined models are noisier and smokier and there is always the chance of fuel spillage, so they are run outdoors, usually on specially-laid tarmac tracks, using tyres etc. as crash barriers. Buggies, both electric and i.c., are also run outdoors on tracks staked out over natural terrain. It would be possible to race electric ones indoors, of course, but much of the fun of buggy racing is in negotiating natural hazards and the vehicles are designed for this purpose.

Over the last few years the cars have become increasingly sophisticated – fully functional suspension, Ackerman steering, differentials, four-wheel drive, clutches and chain, belt, shaft or gear transmission are taken for granted. Selecting the right tyres for the surface and the weather conditions is as important as in full-size racing, as is the setting up the suspension. It is skill in setting up the car, in operating the engine and in actual driving which makes these cars such a challenge. Kits provide all the parts and most can be assembled with a screwdriver, Allen keys and a couple of spanners; there are few scratch-built cars because few amateurs have the skills to match the expertise of the manufacturers. Some kits may seem expensive, but cheaper ones may well require parts to be bought separately which are included in the dearer kits. It is not a cheap hobby, though running costs are not excessive, but it scores in that winning performance cannot be bought and can only be achieved by skill and experience added to a sound basic car.

Starting in R/C

It is not possible to go into detail on every class of car in a book of this type, but since the best choice for the average beginner is likely to be an electric buggy a closer look at this form of vehicle can be taken.

It will be found that electric kits usually include a motor and body shell but not necessarily batteries. The batteries used in all electric cars are nickel cadmium fast charge type and they are often available

The front end of a four-wheel-drive electric buggy, set up to run indoors or on a prepared outdoor surface by the use of smooth tyres. Anti-slip liquids ('goop') are sometimes applied to such tyres.

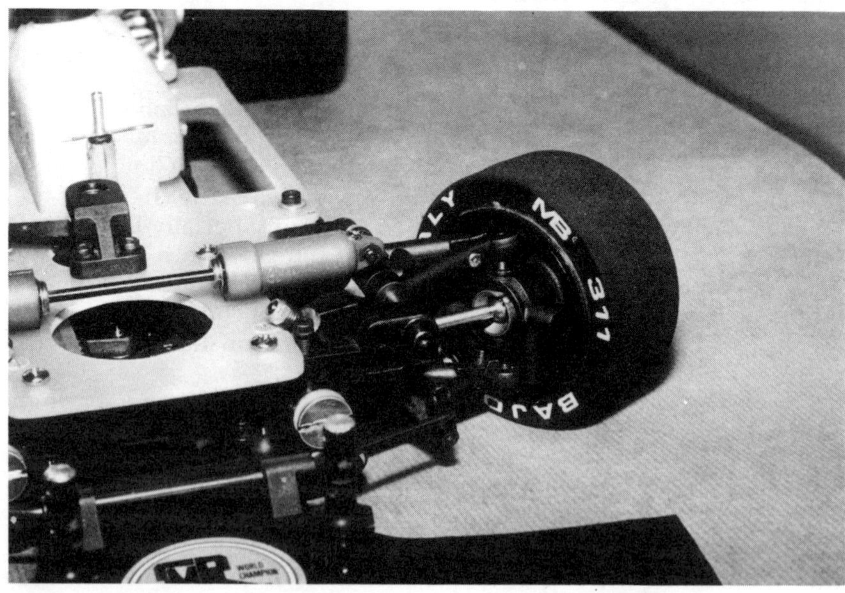

in packs designed to fit specific cars. It is the fast charging capability which has popularised electric cars, since a car can be raced for perhaps 6-7 minutes, put on charge and be ready again in 20 mins. or less where previously one set of batteries would provide only one run per session, needing 14-15 hours to charge. However, be very sure that the cells used are of the vented, fast-charge type and follow charging instructions implicitly to avoid the danger of cells exploding. The currents used may not be high and this can give the feeling that nothing serious can happen, but an exploding cell can cause extensive damage and injury.

There are two basic motor sizes in electric buggies, 380 and 540, usually running off 6 and 7.2 volts respectively. The smaller size is usually provided in simpler and less expensive kits but can give a lively performance; some of the models can be converted to 540 at a later stage. For racing the 540 size is customary, in the form of a Standard Class, where an unmodified and relatively inexpensive motor must be used, or Modified Class, where there is again a limit on motor price but at a level which enables hotter motors to be bought. The 380 Class is recognised for racing, but with only small

An electric buggy – a visible driver head is required by the rules. Speed controller is under the driver and the box in front of him is the steering servo. Motor drives by direct spur gearing on this model.

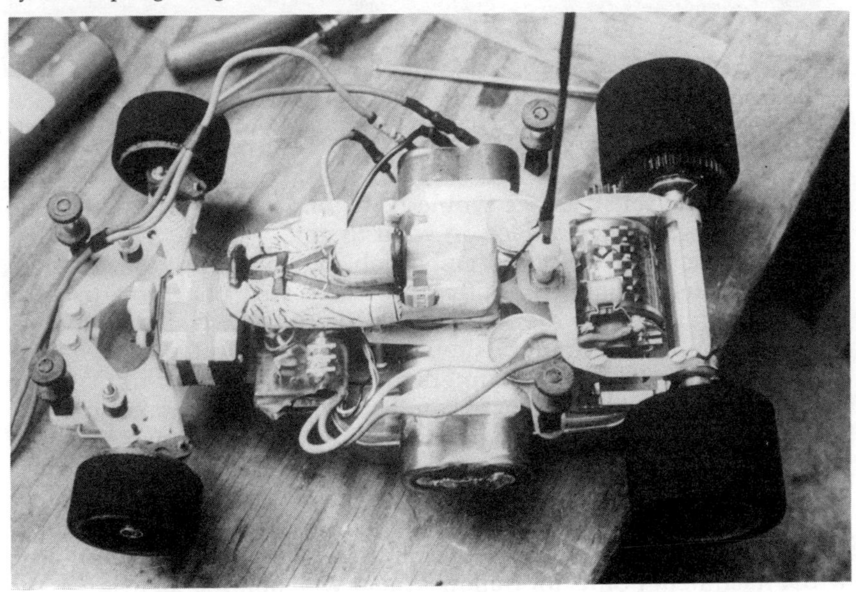

alterations allowed to a basic kit, while Open racing (not an official category) is a no-limit but expensive activity where phenomenal performance is possible, using 8.4 or even 9.6 volt cell packs and, as a general rule, four-wheel drive.

A beginner is advised to buy a 380 or at most a basic Standard 540 kit. The beauty of a buggy is that it can be run in the garden, or in a quiet car park, without noise annoyance to neighbours or the necessity for a specially prepared track, so that someone not within easy reach of a club can still enjoy running. If the intention is to join a club, a kit which can be raced and if necessary upgraded would be a wise

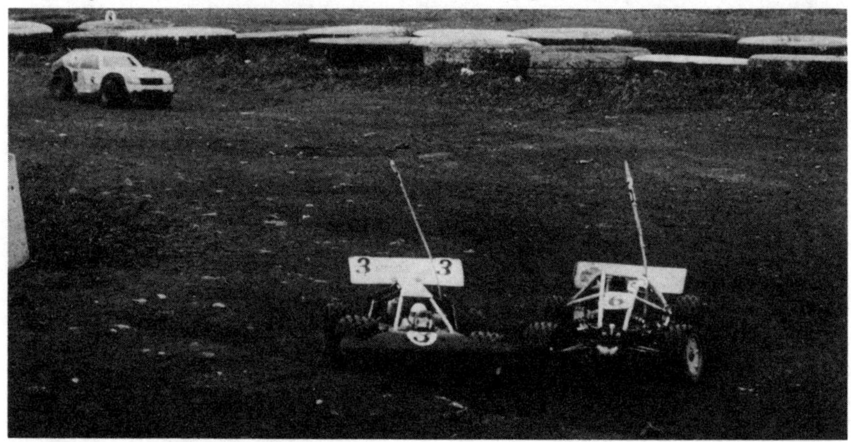

Collision imminent as two electric buggies head for the same spot. Bumps and shunts are common in racing. Vertical wires support the aerials, enabling receivers to respond over greater ranges.

choice, and the sensible step would be to join or at least visit the club before buying, to seek advice on what to get.

The kit itself will be an assembly job, but not one to be rushed. Study the instructions carefully and make sure that you use the specified screws in the right place with the right tools. Screwdrivers, either plain or cross-point, should fit the screws, and the same applies to Allen keys and spanners for socket heads and nuts. Clean off any mould lines (from, for example, ball joints) and make sure that everything goes squarely together the right way round. Incorrect assembly, with resulting stripping and reassembly, is a prime cause of a buggy which doesn't perform to its maximum potential or comes apart somewhere when running.

Most kits supply a moulded plastic chassis of considerable rigidity, with attachment points for trailing arm or wishbone suspension at the front and a swing axle arrangement at the rear. Differentials are normally omitted on 380 buggies, and the simpler ones use all-gear drive to the rear wheels, though shafts, chains or toothed belts may be encountered. There are three basic patterns of tyre, a "sand" type, almost treadless, for smooth surfaces, a conical spiked pattern used mainly on grass, and a general purpose type with a prominent square block pattern. Probably squares, or possibly spikes, will be supplied in the kit; changing tyres is not quite what it may sound, since it is best to glue the tyres to the wheels and an alternative set of tyres thus means buying a further set of wheels.

The chassis will make provision for mounting the motor and drive unit, the battery pack and the radio equipment. Possibly the radio will require its own battery supply, but this will usually depend on the form of speed controller, since more sophisticated ones provide a power take-off point for the radio. Simple speed controllers are electro-mechanical, using a conventional radio servo to move a contact over a switch plate which provides two or three forward speeds and one in reverse. The switch plate is wired with separate circuits incorporating different resistors, using the whole battery all the time. Although this wastes a certain amount of power (in heat through the resistors) it is a better system than using only parts of the battery, giving uneven discharge and consequent recharging problems.

Electronic controllers provide infinitely variable speed in forward and reverse and frequently proportional braking, and they often also include a by-pass switch for full forward speed so that the whole of the power available passes to the motor rather than a small amount being consumed in driving the controller. This type of speed control is costlier, but since it is self-contained and plugs directly into the radio receiver, the price of a separate servo is saved.

Front end steering is exactly like a full-size car, with king pins, radius rods etc. and is operated by a conventional servo, though not quite directly. Normal servos incorporate a train of small gears which, although surprisingly strong, are susceptible to damage if the quite considerable loads on the front wheels are transmitted directly to them; this particularly so if the car hits an obstacle at high speed. The servo is therefore linked to a "servo saver", which is a spring-loaded device capable of absorbing shocks, and the rods operating the wheels are taken from this fitting to the radius arms.

Most kits incorporate some form of protection for the more vulnerable components against water, mud, dust and grit, but thorough and regular cleaning is essential on any R/C car. Additional protection can be achieved by simply clipping the receiver into a plastic bag or rubber balloon and binding the end round the wires leading to or from the receiver with a rubber band. Although an owner running for fun may not drive through puddles or mud patches, dust and grit will still be picked up. The scale of the problem may be judged by the expert opinion that a glowplug engine run without an air filter could be ruined in a quarter of an hour on the average dry track.

Dynamic braking is possible because the motors used in cars are of the permanent magnet type and generate current when the car is moving after the drive current is switched off. If this current is made to work by heating a circuit the load passed back to the motor is considerable and slows the motor and thus the car. This is most noticeable when the drive current is cut off with the car at speed and rapid deceleration results. On an i.c. car a disc or drum brake is used and is normally operated when the throttle is completely closed by an additional spring-loaded over-ride movement of the throttle servo.

Whatever form of springing is used for the suspension, it will tend to have too fast a return rate (unless it is extremely soft) and the car will therefore bounce to an undesirable extent. For more efficient running, and certainly for racing beyond the beginner stage, spring return damping must be fitted and oil-filled dampers are supplied in many of the more up-market kits, or can be bought separately. Experimenting with oil viscosity or, if necessary, adjusting the size of the internal oil bleed hole is part of the setting-up procedure for racing. For fun running it may be enough to fit softer tyres, punctured

Completed chassis and engine, ready for the body panels, of a 1929 'Blower Bentley', modelled to $\frac{1}{15}$ scale by Gerald Wingrove. Every part is meticulously made from the appropriate raw material.

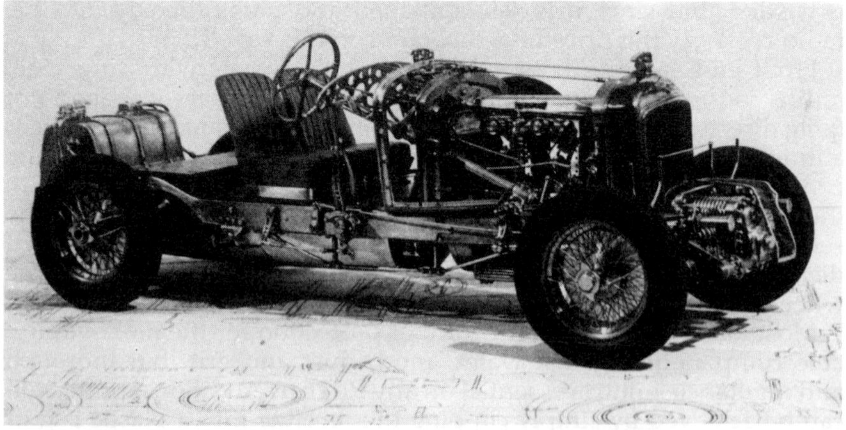

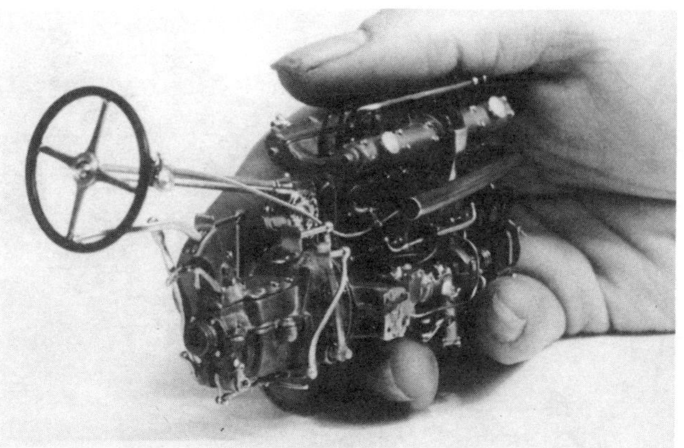

Another Wingrove masterpiece in the making, the engine for a P3 Alfa Romeo to this builders' normal ¹⁄₁₅ scale. Every detail is researched for correct appearance and colour.

so that they do not contain pressurised air, while some owners cut holes in the tyre walls to reduce overall resilience.

Although the foregoing by no means covers the entire subject, most of the salient points have been touched on and enough has been said to demonstrate that modern radio-controlled cars are surprisingly sophisticated. Even though there is little actual construction (compared with building a model from raw materials) there is enormous scope for individual influence on the operation of the vehicle and driving is a skill which takes considerable practice. The challenges offered, and the satisfaction of successfully meeting them, are the reasons for the considerable popularity of R/C cars.

Static models

Although this book, and the television programmes with which it is associated, are primarily concerned with working models, there is general public interest in scale models of cars built as display pieces. Once again the difficulty is likely to be tyres, and short of moulding one's own – which is the course adopted by experts – the type of car, or the scale to which it is built, will usually depend on the availability of suitable tyres from the commercial model or toy field. It is possible to turn tyres on a lathe from, say, rubber boot heels but the tread pattern is difficult to form; wooden tyres are also possible with skilful painting. Wheels may sometimes be turned, or one constructed and used as a plug for a silicon mould to cast a set in resin or low melting-point metal. Spoked wheels have to be built, which is not as difficult as it sounds, though a really neat finish is not easy.

33

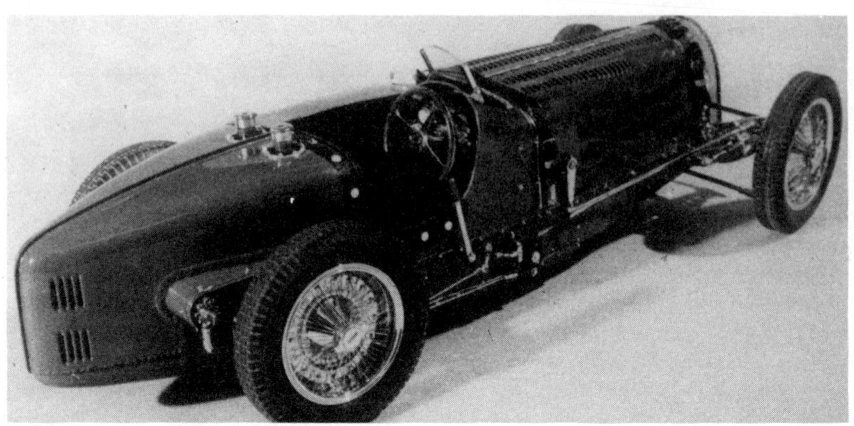

A 1934 Type 59 Bugatti by Wingrove, also at ¹⁄₁₅ scale. Rear wheels each have 80 .22 mm stainless steel spokes!

The rest of the car is best built exactly as the prototype from metal, which means acquiring panel-beating skills. Glass fibre, thin card or moulded polystyrene sheet are alternatives; wood is not favoured by experts because it is difficult to represent the thinness of metal and the crispness of its edges if carved from timber, and getting a car-like paint finish on grainy material without losing overall sharpness poses considerable problems.

Veteran or vintage cars often make a better choice of prototype than vehicles after, say, the mid 1930s, since they usually incorporate simple panel shapes which are less difficult to reproduce than the curved, pressed components of mass-produced bodies. Although they might have more external details these bits and pieces are often of simple form and can be fun to make, even if two or three attempts have to be made. An older car is, in effect, a collection of items which are each fairly straightforward to model and which can usually be finished and painted before assembly. A modern car, on the other hand, relies heavily on its overall shape and finish; it has relatively few excrescences or external details and any part which is finished separately needs to be fitted very closely to retain the overall smoothness of the shape.

Cars, although so much part of the everyday scene in developed countries, are among the most difficult subjects to model well, which undoubtedly contributes to the comparatively low level of activity in this form of modelling and the mere handful of master modellers who over the years have found fame by their outstanding car modelling.

34

Model Boats 3

One would think that, with the thousands of years of development of ships with sails and the long experience of powered vessels which could draw on previous hull development, it would be difficult to make any significant advance in performance with model boats. Yet performance has been improving steadily in both sail and power models over the last sixty years, often hand in hand with simplification. Some of this has been due to the use of newly-evolved materials but most can be accounted for by the growing numbers of enthusiasts involved and the fact that experiments with models are relatively inexpensive and results fairly quick to observe. As a result, a number of successful model innovations have found their way into full-size practice and many members of the full-size industry like to keep abreast of what is happening with models.

Multi-racing – the racing of six or eight R/C models round an M-shaped course for half-hour heats – is a popular modern event. Here four boats head for the camera but a fifth has overdone the turn. Speeds about 40 m.p.h.

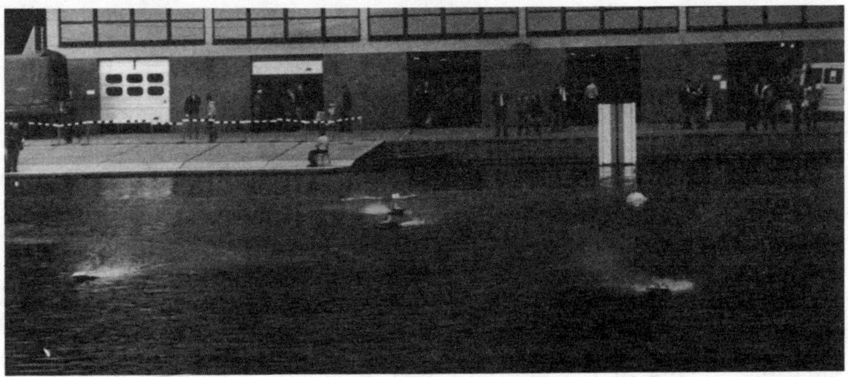

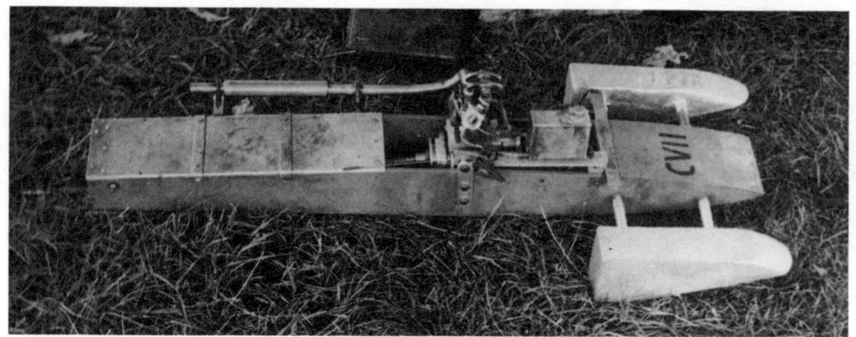

An early hydroplane for tethered running, with a 30 cc hand-built four-stroke petrol engine. This basic shape, with two sponsons at the bow, is still the most commonly used, though with some refinements.

The basic and obvious difference between engine and sail power is that with the former a constant driving force is available in any direction, affected only by wave height and pattern and, in the ultimate, wind strength. With sail the force available for forward propulsion is dependent on wind strength and the direction of the wind in relation to the course required; there is a segment of approximately a quarter circle in which the vessel cannot sail directly to any point at will. Wave height and pattern and limit wind strength are also influences. This fundamental difference outweighs the common factors in hull design to the extent that power and sail must be treated as separate subjects.

Power models

Steam engines for models existed two hundred years ago, to be followed by clockwork and, later, petrol engines and electric motors and even wound rubber strip. As increasing numbers of sailing and power craft appeared on ponds in city parks, clubs came into being, one of the main incentives being that a local authority would provide a private lock-up building for a club, enabling owners to leave models adjacent to the lake. The early clubs around 1870 (and some of them still actively existing) were formed when, apart from railways, there was only horse transport and the advantage of being able to leave models at the lakeside can be imagined.

Apart from occasional articles in publications such as *The English Mechanic* there were no sources of information and clubs provided a valuable means of disseminating knowledge. Sail predominated –

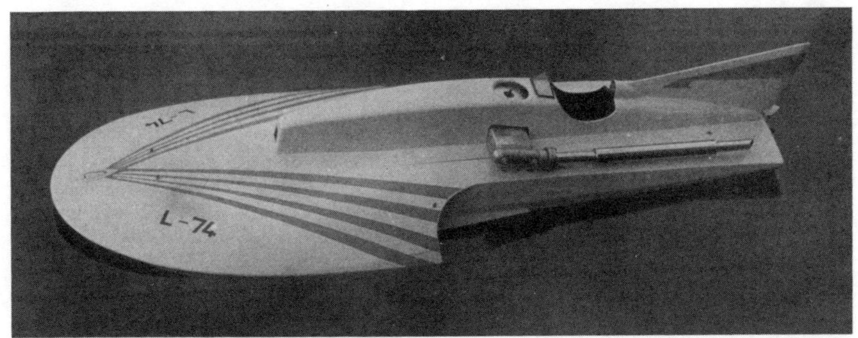

Radio-controlled hydroplanes are popular in the U.S.A. and the hull shapes follow their full-size practice. One difficulty with radio models is the reluctance of this type of hull to turn equally in each direction.

there was the first genuine model magazine, *The Model Yachtsman*, from 1884 to 1894 – but power clubs made progress, accelerated when *The Model Engineer* first appeared in 1898. Petrol engines made an appearance in 1904, though they were not widespread for another 20-25 years, and electric power soon followed, though motors were not very efficient and batteries extremely heavy for the current produced. Steam remained the primary source of power.

Interclub regattas led to the formation of a loose association around 1910, though the nation-wide Model Power Boat Association was not established until 1924. The only other country paralleling this pattern of development was the U.S.A., though there were pockets of activity in Europe, notably in France and Belgium.

The most popular form of competition from the outset was the "steering" event, where models were aimed at a line of buoys about 3 ft. or so apart and about 60 yards from the launch point, scoring for a bull, inner and outer. A variation was to nominate the time one's model would take to cover the course. These and similar tests are still with us under the title "Straight Running".

Club members wading in the lake acted as stoppers, catching the boats at the end of their runs, but as petrol engines developed speeds began to increase; catching a boat doing 20m.p.h. becomes more difficult and even slightly dangerous (12m.p.h. is considered a safe limit). In the late 1920s the practice of tethering fast models to a central pylon and timing them for speed was introduced and a different form of boat, the hydroplane, gradually evolved. These too are still with us, usually referred to as "Tethered Hydroplanes" or "R.T.P. models", R.T.P. being "round the pole" or possibly "round the pylon". Present-day speeds are at a level impossible to conceive

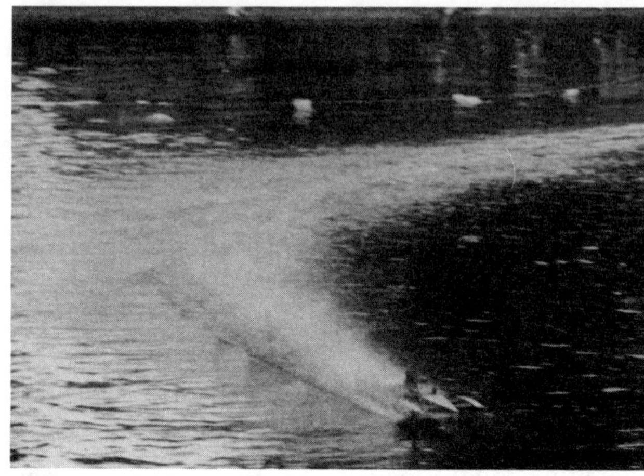

A tethered hydroplane in action. This is the first lap and the engine has not yet 'come in'. Speed is about 60m.p.h. but will increase when fuel balance is reached.

50 years ago – 120-130m.p.h. for the fastest waterscrew hydroplanes and 150-160m.p.h. for a special 2½cc. class with airscrew propulsion.

The biggest change came some 25 years after the formation of the M.P.B.A. with the introduction of radio control equipment which anyone could buy and use. Radio control had been demonstrated in the 1930s and in the immediate post-World War 2 years radio enthusiasts had found boats to be an excellent vehicle for hand-built control equipment, not as difficult to operate and as susceptible to

This is an electric-powered model! A well-known photograph showing German expert Willi Senff conducting trials on a kit model. Speed is high but such boats run only 4-5 minutes per charge.

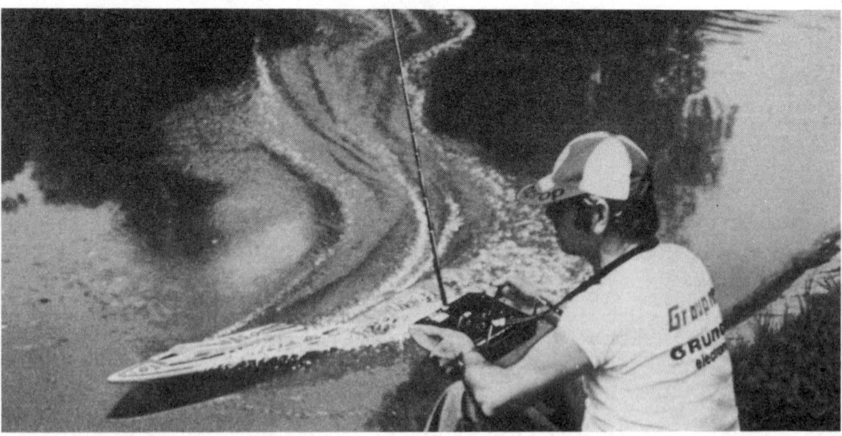

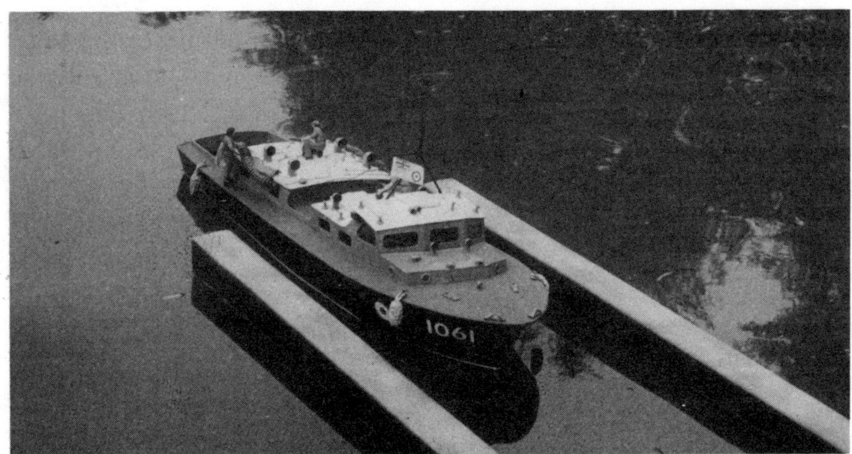

Docking at the end of a steering course is now a regular requirement, the dock width being adjusted for each entrant. This launch-type model is the sort of boat beginners are recommended to try.

damage as aircraft but also not requiring the complexities of wheels and drive mechanisms of cars. Commercial equipment suitable for boat use became available around 1951/2 and there were plentiful supplies of small engines, developed primarily for aircraft but adaptable to or available in marine versions; a whole new aspect of model boating was opened up and was responsible for an enormous expansion of activity.

Competitions for steering round intricate courses and speed round simpler courses grew steadily in popularity, one boat running at a

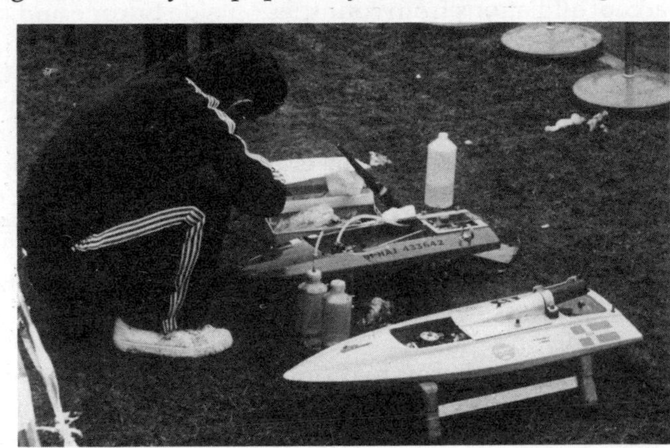

A Swedish entrant working on his model at an international meeting. Multi-racing and speed models follow this general appearance.

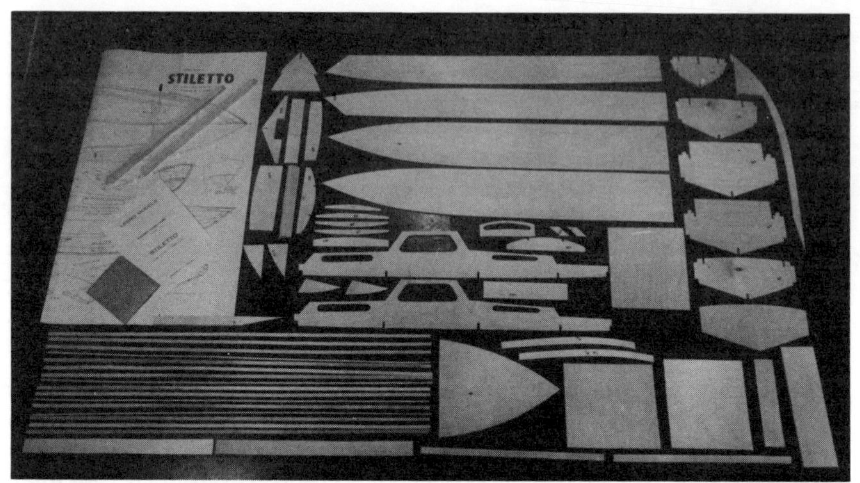

The parts of an all-wood kit for a cabin launch type of model; note the extensive prefabrication. Many modern kits go further and supply a ready-moulded g.r.p. or vacuum-formed styrene hull.

time since this was all that early radio permitted. During the 1960s it became possible to race two boats together and, towards 1970, development of less expensive superheterodyne equipment led to "multi-racing", initially six and later twelve fast models racing simultaneously.

An association of European countries, Naviga, was formed in 1959 but although Britain was nominally a member, it did not assume a major role until after 1967. Around 1980 Naviga was persuaded to accept affiliations from countries outside Europe and, although several major countries such as the U.S.A. are not members, the association seems as near to a world body as we are likely to get. A complication is that some (mainly Eastern European) countries have one national body covering all branches of modelling, a result of which is that Naviga rules include sailing craft when there is already a major world organisation covering yachts, but Naviga sailing events are held separately from power classes, for which there is a major championship meeting held every other year and alternately in east and west Europe. Naviga is generally thought of as a power boat organisation and its classifications and competition courses are used internationally.

Class A is tethered hydroplanes (A1 2½cc, A2 5cc, A3 10cc) and B airscrew hydroplanes (B1 2½cc) on a 31.846m. line (5 laps equals 500m.). C1 to C5 are categories of non-working models, while E are

40

straight runners (EH merchant vessels, EK warships, EX functional). F covers radio (F1 i.c. speed in 3½, 6½ and 15cc sizes plus electric models up to and over 1Kg. weight, F2 is scale ships in three size ranges, F3 steering models, i.c. and electric) and FSR is multi-racing in 3½, 6½, 15cc and a petrol-fuelled class 15-35cc. Additionally there are demonstration/novelty events for both teams and individual operators. This makes a total of 28 classes (five of which are non-working) and at a championship the average entry is usually over 20 per class plus perhaps another 5 per class in junior entries, in other words over 700 boats participating in a week of competitions.

Sport boating

Not everyone is interested, or can take part, in competitions and it is estimated that for every club member there are at least twenty model boat owners who just enjoy running a boat, which gives a six-figure total in the U.K. alone. The majority of these boats are electric powered, of scale appearance and radio-controlled, though there are several thousands fitted with diesel or glowplug engines and radio and these tend to be of the hard chine launch type. A hard chine hull has a definite corner where the bottom panels meet the sides and can therefore consist of a light framework covered with sheets of thin ply rather than having to be carved from a laminated block or planked with individual narrow planks.

Scale models can represent innumerable types of ships. This charming paddle tug not only looks and performs well but it is a living portrait displaying the working appearance of a vessel no longer used.

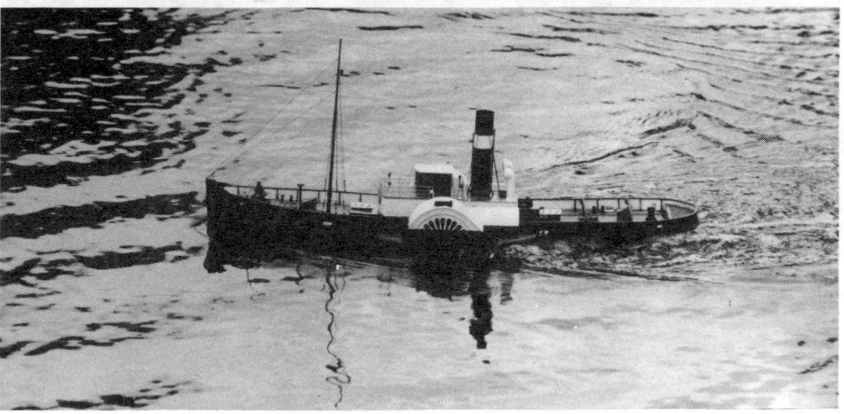

As it happens, the hard chine form, which is relatively simple, quick and inexpensive to build, is also the best for fast models, while plywood is generally fairly easily available and consistent in quality. Most of the published designs and most of the kits sold between, say, 1950 and 1970 were of this type. However, in the late 1950s glass fibre (more correctly, glass reinforced plastic or g.r.p.) began to be used for hulls and ten years or so later vacuum-formed polystyrene hulls started to appear. Either saves the necessity to build a hull and neither is limited to hard chine form.

There has always been interest in scale ship models but at a fairly low level because of the necessity of making all the fittings and the cost of suitable timber even if it could found. With few exceptions working scale ships were not of a very high standard even thirty years ago in Britain, though some excellent models were being made on the Continent, especially in Eastern European countries where radio control could not be bought and engines were scarce but car heater and windscreen motors could be adapted to drive models. Few British modellers had seen these models before the first large party attended the 1967 European Championships, to be stunned by the quality of the scale ships.

The awakened interest and the possibilities of moulded hulls, reinforced by increasing numbers of scale models in kit form, engendered a growth of activity in scale boats which continues to the

Smaller motors (3½-5 cc) in speed models are often geared down to keep propeller rotation to under 20,000 r.p.m. This German model also uses flexible engine mountings to reduce total noise output.

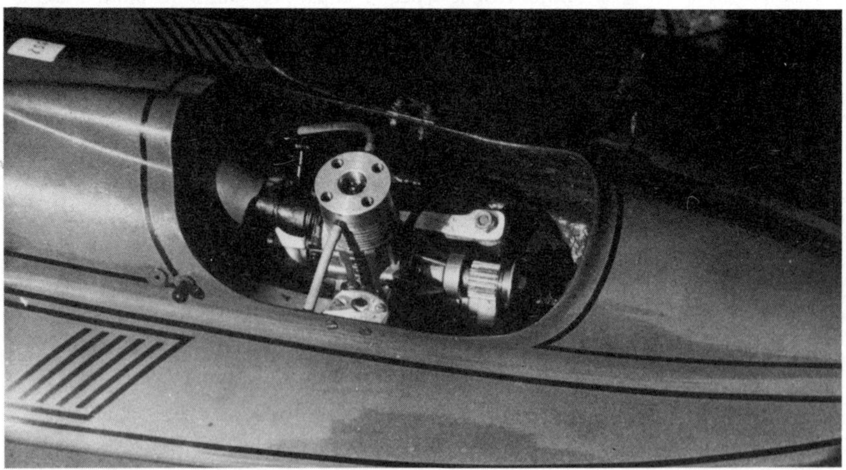

present, and the standards achieved by modellers and in recent kit production in Britain are now the equal of anywhere.

Interest in functional competition categories in any sport tends to remain high while progress is apparent, but as improvement becomes more difficult the class often gets left to a handful of experts. To some extent this has been happening in power boating and has contributed to the upswing of activity in scale modelling.

All of this has benefited the average sport modeller, who most often prefers his model to identify with a full-size prototype. Scale plans, kits and moulded hulls give him a wide choice, and the overall level of demand has enabled the model trade to come forward with fittings and accessories at reasonable prices. It has also ensured competition in the price of radio control equipment, which in real terms costs about a fifth of what was paid thirty years ago, and, further, radio has made possible the use of stretches of water which could not be used for non-radio boats, which require access at any point of a lake bank.

Clubs and official bodies have fairly strict silencing and safety rules and mandatory insurance; loss of control, even momentarily, of a fast model can cause damage or injury, while excessive noise nuisance can quickly lead to the loss of the use of a lake. Those who run a boat for fun should take heed of this, and not only if they run fast i.c.-engined boats. Spectators can trip on equipment or receive injury from a transmitter aerial, which might give grounds for a substantial claim.

Beginners

A power boat is a good choice for someone starting in modelling, since it need not take too long to build, requires little in the way of special tools or workspace, is comparatively inexpensive and is unlikely to suffer serious damage in use. If a radio is bought for it, it can be used in other models and will last for several years with care.

There is considerable variation in people's approach to a new hobby. Some will be prepared to pay £100 for a kit and others want to spend as little as possible, some will be more anxious to get the boat on the water and some will enjoy building. There are all-wood kits where everything has to be built from pre-shaped parts or, at the other extreme, those with formed g.r.p. or polystyrene hulls and complete sets of finished fittings. The difference is reflected in the price and, usually, the time required to complete the model, as naturally the more the manufacturer has done for you the higher the

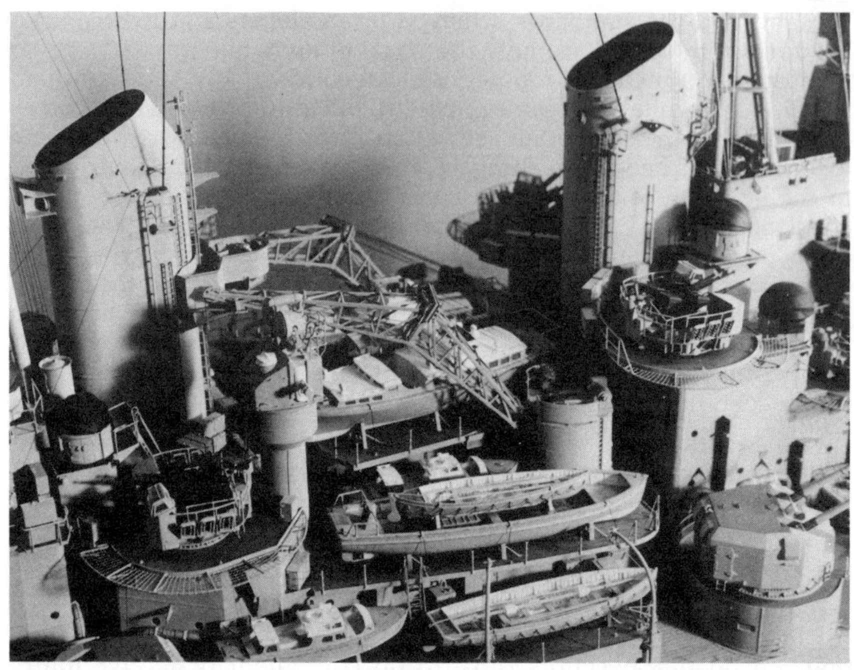

Detail from Alex MacFadyen's H.M.S. *Vanguard* gives some idea of the enormous amount of work needed to build a warship model. Most scale modellers settle for a smaller prototype like a trawler or, if looking for the unusual, a vehicle ferry such as in the picture below.

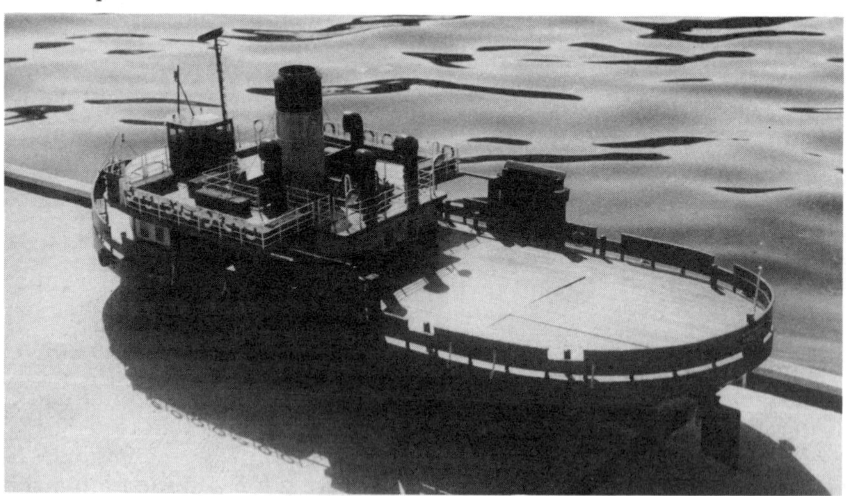

price he must charge. Most good model shops will be prepared to show you the contents of a kit and advise on its complexity.

The alternative is to build from a plan, of which there is a very wide selection. They can be bought, or *Model Boats* magazine includes free full-size plans from time to time and many of these are suitable for a beginner. Parts have to be traced and transferred to the wood and cut out, but this does not really take all that long. A small and simple model is included in this book; it is a little on the small side, due to the constraints of page size, but it will provide practice and will perform well on small ponds.

Normal advice is to choose something very simple and of reasonable size for a first model. Component parts are larger and there is more room to work in if a model of, say, 25-30 in. length or more is built, rather than an 18 in. one. This applies particularly if radio is to be fitted, where room to move makes installation a great deal easier.

If electric power is used, it is well worth the extra cost of nickel-cadmium (nicad) batteries, which will last for years; 3,000 charge/discharge cycles is quite normal, and they will tolerate a degree of neglect which makes them very little trouble to look after. The single most important point with an electric boat is accurate alignment of the motor and propeller shaft so that there is no friction whatsoever. This gives best speed and longest battery life and saves wear on the motor and prop-shaft bushes. Dashing around at full speed flattens batteries fairly quickly – dry batteries may only last a minute or two unless they are relatively big ones – but at about half speed they are likely to last

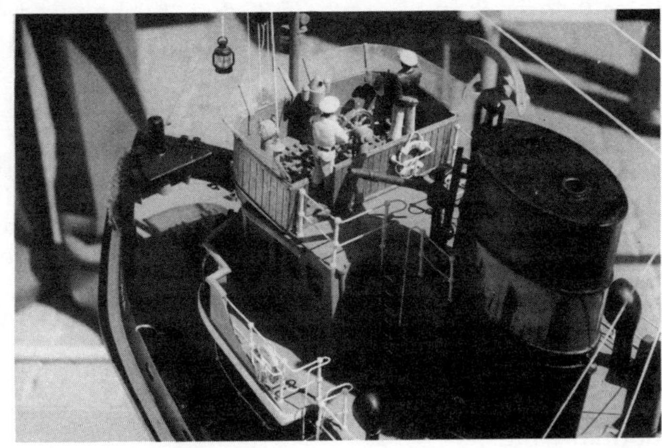

Tugs are ever-popular scale subjects. This 4 ft. model of *Ionia* includes the skipper and mate on the open bridge – a nice touch!

about three times as long. A switching or speed control system operated by the radio is normally used.

When a diesel or glowplug engine is used familiarisation with starting and running should be obtained by mounting the engine in a test stand, or bolting it in a cut-out in a piece of hard wood clamped in a vice or screwed to a bench, so that technique can be practised. This can save a lot of frustration at the lakeside. These engines are not usually difficult to run if the operator has enough experience to recognise what is wrong, and this can only come from practice. Once again, alignment of motor and prop-shaft is very important – with no fuel, it should be possible to "bounce" the piston against compression by twisting the propeller.

As with other types of modelling, interested readers are recommended to read as much as they can find on the subject since it has only been possible to touch on a few matters in these pages. Again, the experience of club members is freely available and an invaluable aid to overcoming any queries or problems which might arise for a beginner.

Sailing models

At least 98% of model sailing craft are Bermuda-rigged, that is with two triangular fore and aft sails (jib and main) fitted with booms at the foot. As with full-size, experience has shown this to be the most efficient form of rig and the one which gives sailing closest to the wind, allowing a vessel to sail to windward (i.e. upwind) in a series of tacks. A square-rig model (sails across the hull) is unlikely to be able to sail closer than perhaps 75-80 deg. to the wind direction and the leeway it makes (the speed with which it is blown sideways) effectively means that its track will be at 90 deg. or more to the wind, or in other words it will not make any progress to windward. Full-size square riggers could do a little better than this, but only a little!

Sailing vessels are most affected by what is called the cube law. If it is desired to make a 1/10 scale model the *length* will be 1/10 of the original. The sails will be 1/10 of the foot measurement and 1/10 the height, so the *area* will be 1/100. In the case of the hull the length is 1/10, the beam 1/10 and the depth 1/10, so the *volume* is 1/1000. Since the weight of a floating body equals the weight of the volume of water displaced, it is not possible to increase stability by adding weight without distorting the hull shape, which means that a true scale model is unlikely to be sufficiently stable to sail in normal winds.

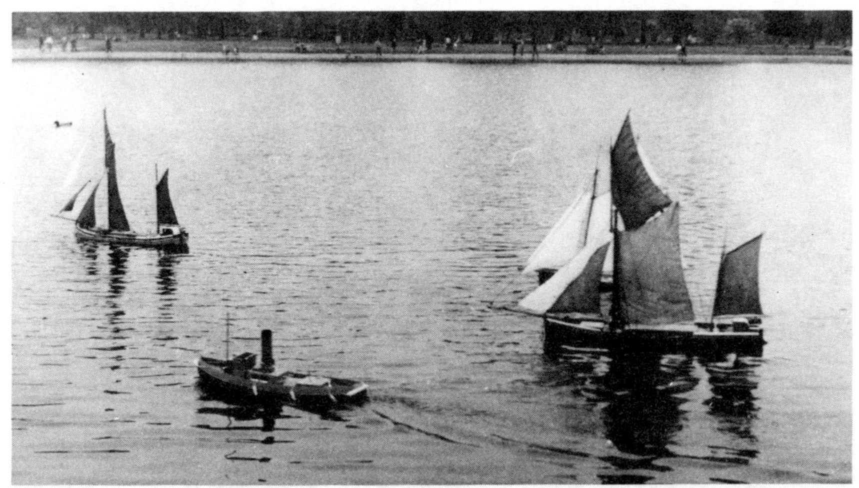

Above, three of the contestants in a Thames barge sailing race. These models are ¼₄ scale, about 4 ft or so hull length. An electric T.I.D. tug fusses by in the foreground. Below, close racing as RM class yachts turn in light wind to beat out to a mark.

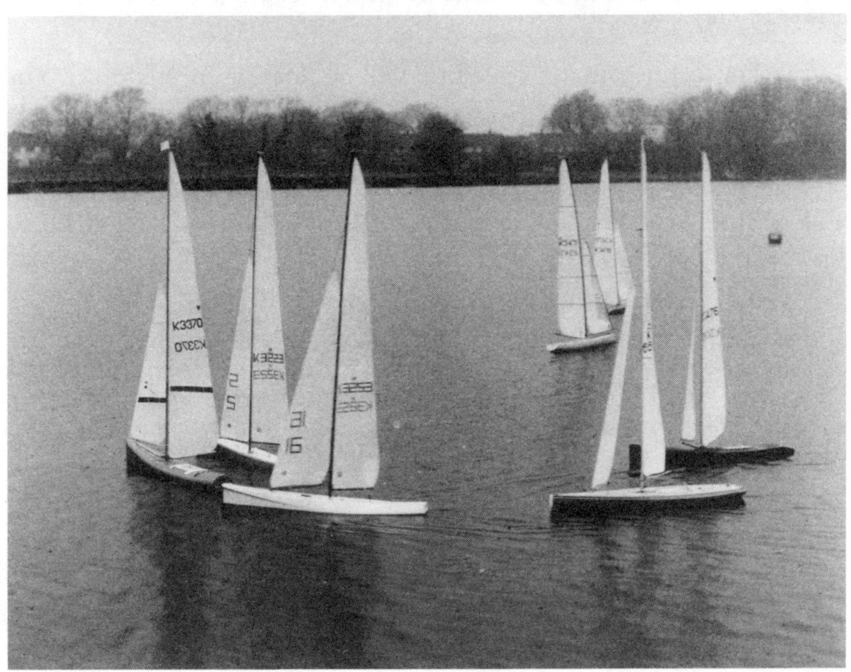

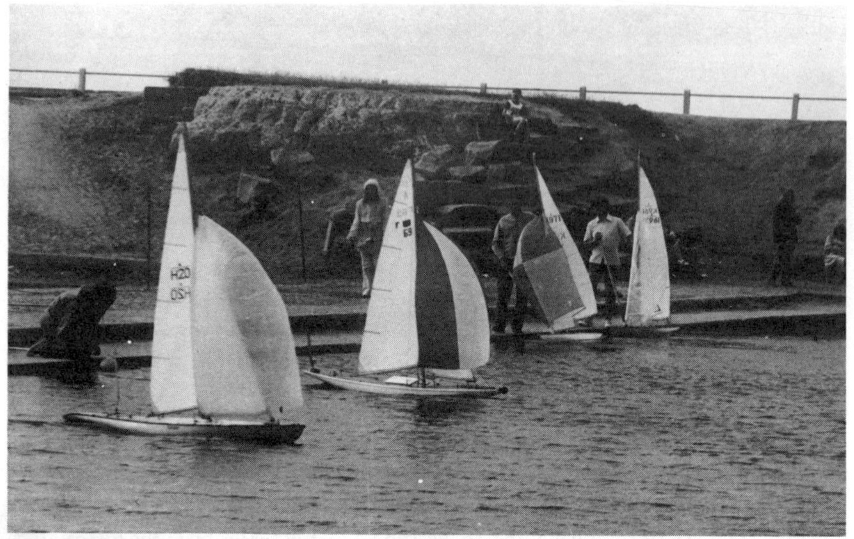

A pair of A class yachts start a run: the next pair stands ready. Spinnakers are used on vane-steered yachts but rarely with radio. The A is the largest model yacht class, may be 60-70 lbs in weight.

Another factor is that a scale hull will be floating in the top two or three inches of water where resistance to sideways motion is less. It is recognised that the smaller a model the deeper its keel must be, relatively, in order for it to get an adequate "grip" to prevent excessive leeway. The usual practice with a scale sailing model is to add a false keel for sailing purposes, improving its resistance to sideways movement and allowing ballast weight to be carried at the bottom of the keel to improve stability.

Coupled with the delicacy of details and complexity of the rigging and sail adjustment, the foregoing explains why few accurate models of sailing vessels are seen afloat and why most successful ones are large-scale models of small fore and aft rigged prototypes. There *are* some excellent models of clippers and brigs and the like, but even their patient and skilful builders will admit to sailing limitations.

Yachts divide into those built to specific racing classes, raced either under radio control or with automatic vane steering mechanisms, and those built for sport sailing, many of which make some concessions to scale appearance by including a coachhouse and/or cockpit, pulpits and rails and other visual but non-functional embellishments. Many sport models nowadays employ radio control, but there is still a lot of pleasure and satisfaction to be had from learning to trim a free-sailing

48

model. It is possible to make a simple vane gear for even quite small yachts to add to the degree of control and the fascination of sailing.

It is not always realised that a yacht's course is determined by the setting of its sails and that the rudder should never be used except for turning or just an occasional minor course correction to keep the sails full. Application of rudder slows the boat down if more than 1-2 degrees of movement is used. It follows that to sail a model under radio control there must be control of the sail sheets and the rudder; it is possible to set the sails in one position and steer the yacht by rudder only, but the boat will only sail properly on the course for which that particular sail setting is correct. To sail efficiently on any course calls for the sail setting to be infinitely adjustable, for both sails, between, say, 3 and 90 deg. to the hull centre line.

The ideal relative setting of the two sails is for the jib to be approximately 2 degrees further out than the mainsail at any setting, and this makes possible "synchronous sheeting" where one control adjusts both sails simultaneously. The usual system is to use a sail winch to drive a long loop of line (the sheeting line) stretched along the hull just above the deck, or sometimes under the deck. One line from each boom (the sheet) passes through a central eye immediately below the attachment point on the boom and is then led across and

The smallest official yacht class is the 36 in. Restricted, two vane examples of which are about to be started on a beat in this picture. Radio control is currently becoming popular in this class.

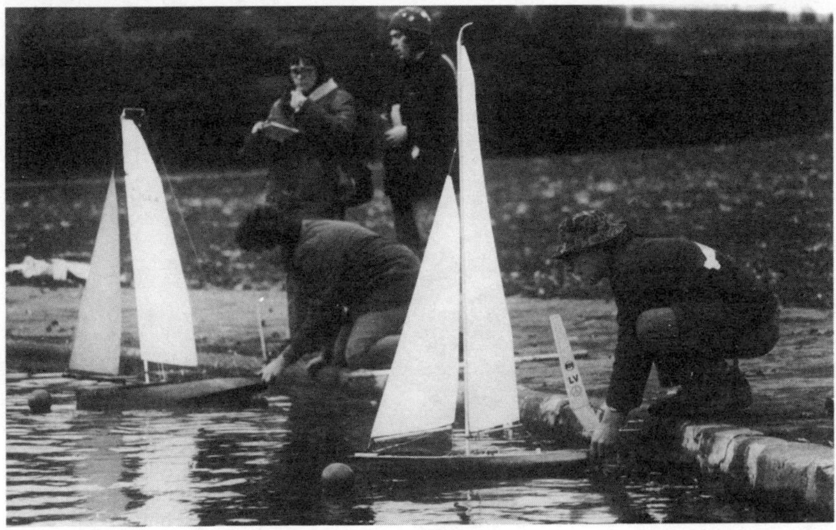

made fast on one side of the sheeting line. Fore and aft movement of the sheeting line thus moves both sheets an equal amount and if the sheets are attached to the boom at equal distances from the boom pivot points, both booms will swing through exactly the same angle. Their relative positions at any angle thus remain the same.

In order for the yacht to sail properly the centre of effort of the sails must balance against a point on the hull called the centre of lateral resistance. If the centre of effort is too far forward the yacht will turn away from the wind, if too far aft it will keep turning into wind and stopping. To get it in the right position the mast is moved bodily fore and aft and provision for this adjustment is always made in a "proper" design. The test is for the yacht to sail straight, without using the rudder, for a good distance (about 50 yards) with the mainsail at 5 deg. and the jib 7 deg. from the hull centre line. At these settings the boat should sail at 40-45 deg. to the wind. A pleasant afternoon can be spent in tuning a yacht to do this consistently.

Most racing yachts need to be tuned very carefully for maximum speed on any heading, since the rules controlling their design have the intended effect of equalising performance, the two major factors in which are sail area and hull waterline length. Yachts are administered internationally by the International Model Yacht Racing Union and the classes used are world-wide. In all but one recently-introduced class the same general specifications are used for both vane steered and radio yachts, the difference in control being signified by 'R' in front of the classification. In order of size they are:

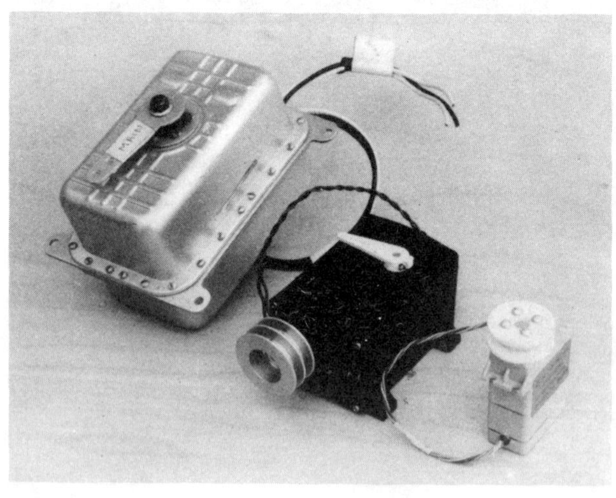

Sheet winches for radio yachts. The large one is what many boats started with and the smallest is what is used today.

36R (R36R). Basically a British class, but built elsewhere. Length 36in., max. weight 12lbs., sail area unlimited but hull must fit in a box 36x9x11in.

Marblehead (M,RM). The most popular international class for both vane and radio. Length 50 in., sail area 800 sq. in. No other major restrictions. Usually about 10-16 lbs. displacement.

6 metre (6m, R6m). Not nowadays widely sailed, this is based on the full-size 6m rule. About 54 in. long, 1000 sq. in. of sail and 18-22 lbs., but can vary depending on how rule is used.

EC12m. A one-design radio class 59 in. long, 26 lbs., which must use a g.r.p. hull from an approved supplier.

10-rater (10r, R10R). Second most popular class, based on a simple formula relating length and sail area so that increase of one decreases the other. Average 58-60 in. waterline, 12-1300 sq. in. of sail, 16-24 lb. Overall length in excess of 6 ft.

A (RA). The largest class, with a fairly complex rule allowing wide variation but equal performance. Average 40-50 lb., around 52-54 in. waterline and 6 ft. plus length, sail 14-1500 sq. ins.

Methods of racing

Vane races entail each boat sailing every other on a tournament system, ideally first to windward (3 pts.) and then to leeward (2 pts.) so that a race consists of a stream of pairs of yachts tacking up the lake, then running with spinnakers down the lake. Radio racing involves from 6 to 12 yachts racing round a triangular course, two laps, or sometimes an Olympic-type course with a triangular first lap and a "sausage" second lap. Sailing rules are virtually identical with full-size rules, including a milling start with a one-minute countdown. Heats may be to an all-in schedule or the entries may be divided into three or four or more 8-boat fleets with the two top boats in each heat moving up and the two bottom ones moving down.

Very wide use is made of g.r.p. hulls and, in top racing, materials such as carbon fibre, Kevlar, Mylar etc. There are, however, still many enthusiasts who prefer building to racing and some very fine wood hulls are seen. Planking (carvel building) is normally used but there are large numbers of hard chine yachts built in ply and some chine boats have consistently appeared in the first half dozen in major races, including World Championships.

Laymen are invariably astonished at the weight of the ballast bulb or casting. A chunk of lead of more than 40 lbs. (18Kg) in weight, not uncommon on an A class yacht, is bound to cause someone to ask if it won't sink the yacht! Surprise is also expressed at the fact that a majority of skippers have their sails made for them and that a racing yacht will often have at least four suits of sails, of decreasing area, to cope with all wind conditions.

Beginning

Any boat, model or full-size, always looks much larger out of the water than in it. A 36 in. yacht may look huge to a newcomer when it is in the workshop, but it looks very small afloat. Beginners are recommended to choose a 36 in. model, or, at the smallest, a 30 in. one, if they envisage installing radio, or even for free-sailing. The bigger the yacht the better it is likely to sail and the easier it can be to build, while the actual cost will not be considerably greater, at least if it is built from a plan. Choose a straightforward hard chine design which includes all construction details and fittings; most round bilge designs are shown as "lines only" and a beginner would need to obtain a book explaining how to build a yacht from this type of drawing.

It is possible to obtain g.r.p. hull shells, but a drawing or book will still be needed to fit one of these out. Help and advice are available from club members and it may be possible to buy a second-hand yacht through a club. There are also kits, often with vacuum-formed or g.r.p. hulls and ready-finished sails and fittings. Some of these kits are of scale appearance but do not fit in any particular class, or there are kits for 36R and Marblehead class racing yachts. If you think you may join a club and participate in an occasional race it is obviously necessary to build a yacht in one or other of the classes, and it is advisable to find out beforehand what classes are raced in the local club.

Running costs for a yacht are virtually nil, but there is a great deal to learn in this aspect of modelling. With no noise and no pollution, sailing craft are acceptable on many waters barred to other forms of boating, and they are unlikely to become severely damaged or to wear out. All these factors contribute to making them attractive. On the other side of the scale, few model shops stock fittings or accessories and the would-be builder thus has to rely on mail order for specialist items or make them himself, which is not as difficult as it may sound. Everything needed to make a yacht is easily available, but not necessarily in the corner shop.

52

Model Aircraft

Model aircraft seem to get more publicity than other types of models, perhaps because they are more easily visible, or there are more of them or, because they move in three dimensions, there is a touch more "magic" about them. There is always the chance of a spectacular crash, so beloved of press and T.V. camera wielders and of editors who presumably think that the writing-off of possibly months of work demonstrates human eccentricity. Perhaps it does, and an aeromodeller has to be prepared for an occasional pile-up or at least some damage, or even a fly-away model, but to balance this are the scores of models which survive for several seasons and provide a never-ending source of pleasure and satisfaction to their owners.

The first successful flying machines were model gliders (if one discounts lighter-than-air vehicles, balloons etc.) but powered models also made flights before full-size aircraft, with limited success with steam power in the 1840s but sufficiently successful with rubber power in the 1870s for models to be sold. Rubber strip was the

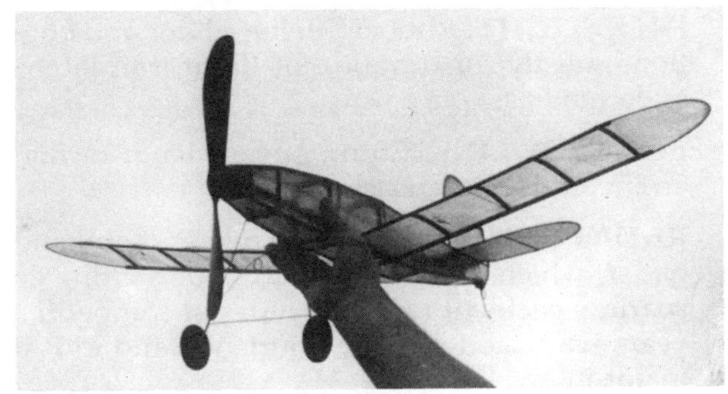

Oiled silk covering on a spruce, birch and bamboo frame was normal up till the mid-1930s. This *Kinglet* was a popular design.

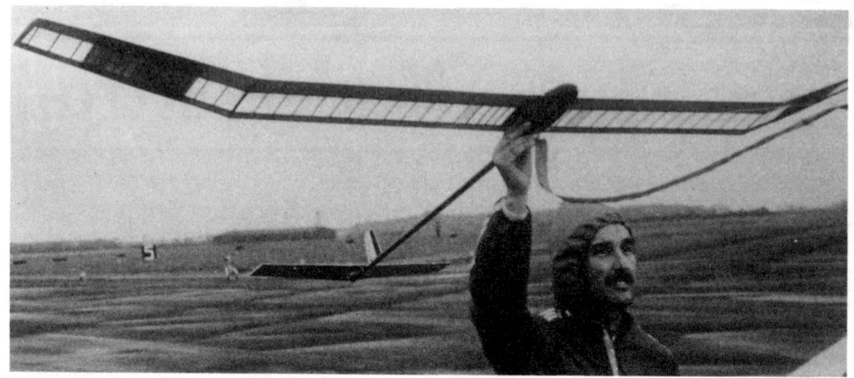

Gliders are towed up on a 50m towline. This example is to the A2 class, the most popular international category for free flight. Streamer on line enables release to be seen and line wound in untangled.

standard form of power right into the 1930s, although petrol engines and compressed air motors were very occasionally used from about 1904 onward. The (relatively) miniature petrol engine made commercially appeared in the early 1930s, as did towline gliders. During World War 2 control-line flying started in the U.S.A. and "diesels", compression ignition engines, were developed in several European countries; glowplug ignition appeared in the 1940s in America. Early radio model experiments were taking place around 1936 but practical commercial equipment did not start to be widely available until about 1950.

The pattern of aeromodelling has remained basically the same for about 30 years, with three broad categories, but detail differences within each category have been marked as techniques have developed and new materials and concepts have been introduced. The three basic areas are:

FREE FLIGHT. Rubber power, glider and engine power. Competitions mostly for duration of flight, but lately a strong interest in scale models.

CONTROL-LINE. Stunt, speed, team racing, combat, and again an increasing interest in scale.

RADIO CONTROL. Engine power (aerobatics, pylon racing) and glider, which sub-divides into slope soaring and thermal (flat field) soaring, each with various types of competition. Over the past few years scale models have flourished and in R/C power are now the major interest.

54

Free flight

A major change in rubber models occurred with the introduction of balsa about 1930. English reaction was that tissue-covered balsa models were unsuited to the climate, but in only a few years they had replaced the spruce, bamboo, wire and oiled silk models which had been the previous norm. The folding propeller, twin or single blade and the dethermaliser (a device for bringing a model quickly but safely down after a predetermined time) were other major developments, although free-wheeling and even feathering propellers are still frequently used. Geared motors have been used off and on, as have retracting undercarriages, and there have been many small technical refinements. The luck element has been reduced by the imposition of a maximum time, often 3 mins. but depending on weather conditions, and five competition flights. Fly-offs take place between any models which have recorded five "maximums".

Gliders, or sailplanes, are towed up on a 50m. line and techniques have developed to enable the model to be held circling on the towline until evidence of rising air appears. Five maxes. are regularly achieved in reasonable conditions, leading to a fly-off.

The oldest competition is the Wakefield Trophy, for rubber models, going back nearly 60 years. Note slim fuselage, two-blade folding propeller and anti-warp construction of this modern model.

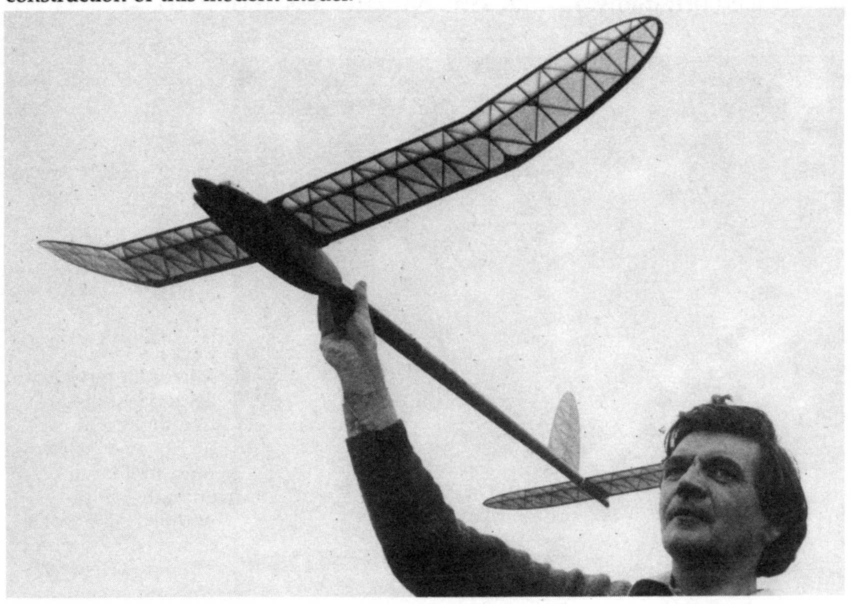

Power models have a phenomenal climb rate, straight up, and they could be out of sight in a clear sky on a 20 second engine run. Even on the 10 or sometimes 7 sec. run allowed they reach an amazing height. Modern techniques may include a timer which stops the engine and at the same time repositions the tailplane and possibly rudder for the best glide; the same timer may trip the d.t. (dethermaliser) or a second timer may be carried. Some even have wings which fold in half to increase climb rate, the folded-under tip sections flipping out to full span as the motor stops. Again, five maxes followed by a fly-off is the usual pattern.

These models usually comply with international rules on wing area, weight, engine size, rubber weight etc. laid down by the model section of the Federation Aeronautique Internationale, the world body, but many rubber, glider and power models are built for fun flying only and most kits are in this category. Such models are much more docile and, apart from rubber models, length of flight can be increased by using a longer engine run or a longer towline.

There are other, national, rules for competitions or they may be "open", for any size of model, and there are competitions for chuck gliders (smallish all-balsa models thrown from the hand) and CO_2 models. These last use small engines running on compressed carbon dioxide gas, usually obtained from soda siphon bulbs, which were introduced originally around 1948 but after a year or two disappeared;

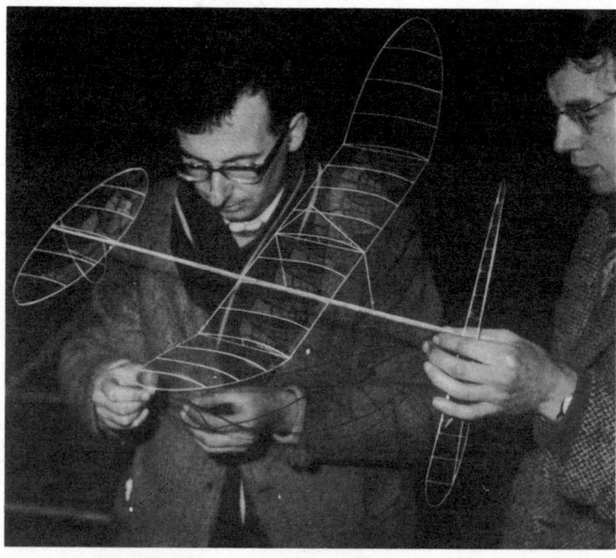

Microfilm models are a specialist area of free flight and can fly for over half-an-hour in a large enough hall on perhaps 3000 turns of the rubber motor. They fly at barely walking speed.

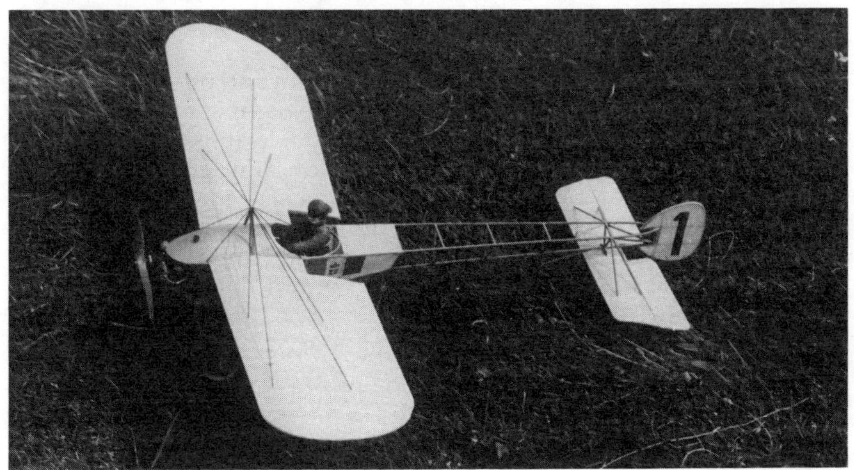

Many small scale models such as this Bleriot are powered by CO_2 motors, the commonest of which will fly models of 20-24 in. span. Six or seven flights can be given by one soda siphon gas bulb.

recently they have made a reappearance and have a strong following for free flight sport and scale models as well as both outdoor and indoor competitions.

Indoor flying requires a large hall, the best site in Britain being one of the vast airship hangars at Cardington. The elite among indoor models are rubber-powered microfilm designs, which are incredibly light and fragile aeroplanes covered with a very thin film produced by pouring a dope-like solution on water, allowing it to spread out and dry, then picking it up on a wire or thin wood frame ready to apply. A

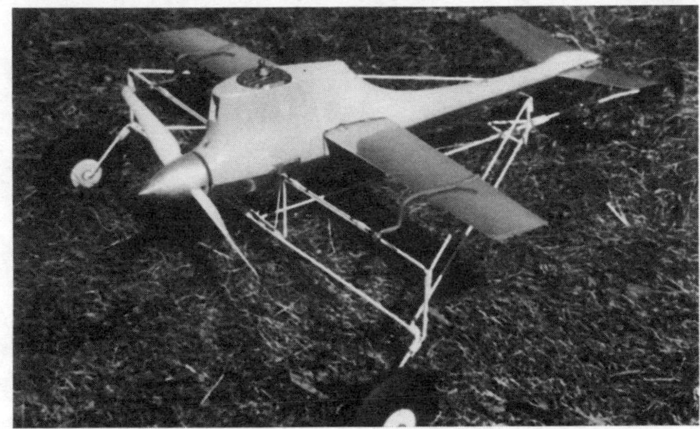

Control-line speed models are tiny and do not have an undercarriage. Instead they take off from a 'dolly' which remains on the ground. Even the smallest class will fly at over 100 m.p.h.

30 in. model will weigh only one or two grammes and with expert trimming may fly for over 30 minutes.

Other, simpler models, some using microfilm and others specifying tissue are also flown indoors, as are lightweight chuck gliders. A totally different category is small scale models (e.g. Peanut scale, limited to 13 in. span) which are usually flown in large sports halls and leisure centres. Smaller halls can be used for electric R.T.P. (round the pole) flying, with models fitted with electric motors fed through their tether lines with current from a car battery or mains transformer; the flier varies the current with a hand controller and limited aerobatics are possible.

Control line flying

Originally known as "U-Control", c/l flying entails two lines of up to as much as 110 ft. (for large models) connecting the model to a handle. In the model the lines are attached to a bell-crank which turns movement through 90 deg. and, basically, operates the model's elevators through a stiff wire push-rod. Thus movement of the handle gives up or down elevator: the "pilot" controls the model in pitch as he turns to remain facing it as it flies in a circle of which he is the centre. It takes a little practice to fly well and to avoid dizziness.

Three stunt fliers with typical models. The centre one has a 'profile' fuselage and all three have wing flaps, essential for the square-cornered stunts required in the full official stunt schedule.

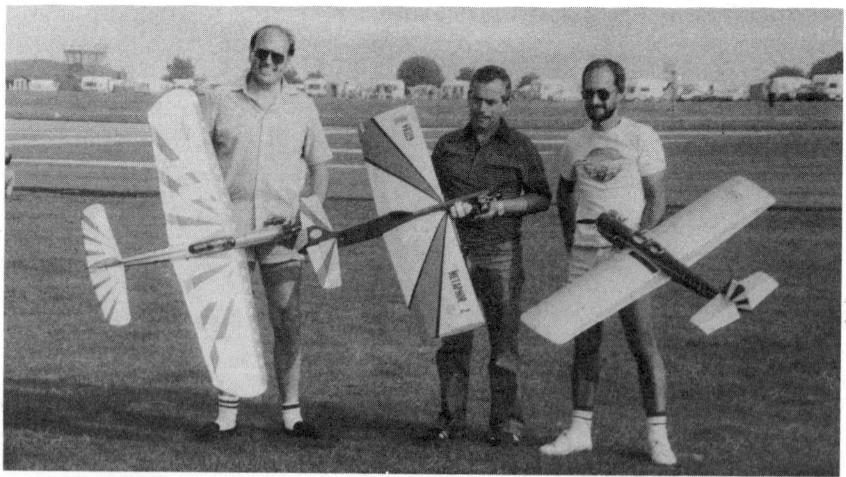

Small and light models can use twine lines but steel wire is better, and seven-strand steel wire is usually used for serious flying. There is a system using a single wire but this has never become generally used. A third line is sometimes added for further control, usually of the engine throttle, placed centrally between the main lines so that handle movement does not affect its length. This extra line is usually operated by a trigger, the aircraft end being spring biased. For added manoeuvrability a second push-rod is taken off the bell-crank to operate flaps on the wing trailing edge; these flaps move in the opposite direction to the elevators (i.e. flaps up with down elevator) and have the effect of tightening loops etc. on stunt models.

Stunt flying is the most popular for individual modellers. Any manoeuvre in the vertical plane – loops, bunts, figure 8s, top hats and many others – can be carried out with a suitable model, which will be quite large and lightly built compared with a trainer. The latter will be robust and limited perhaps to loops and wing-overs (the model flying half the circle vertically). Speed models are comparatively small and can be unorthodox in appearance, but capable of speeds in excess of 150 m.p.h. A pole with a swivelling stirrup is mounted in the centre of the circle, the flier having to place his wrist in the stirrup so that he cannot influence the model's speed by whipping or leading the model. At high speeds some agility is required!

A typical combat model at an international meeting (left) flown by a Chinese team. Right, team race pilots in action. Flying three models in one circle requires rules on overtaking etc.

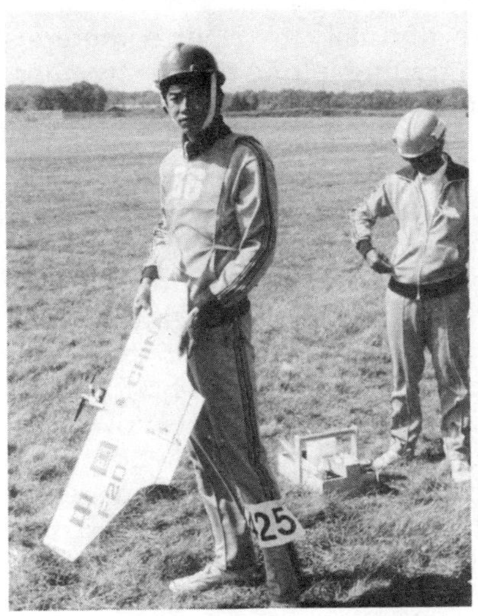

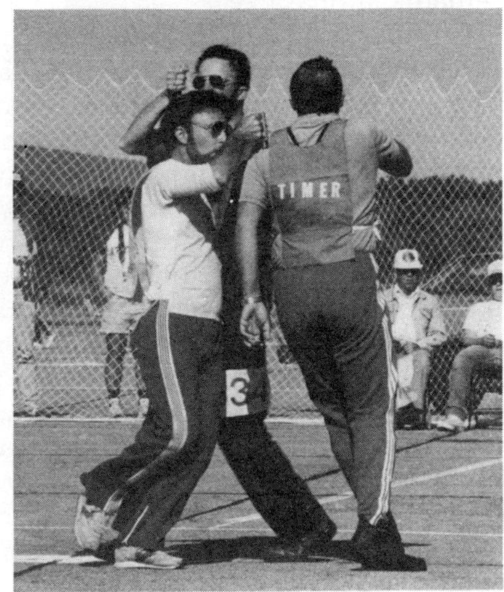

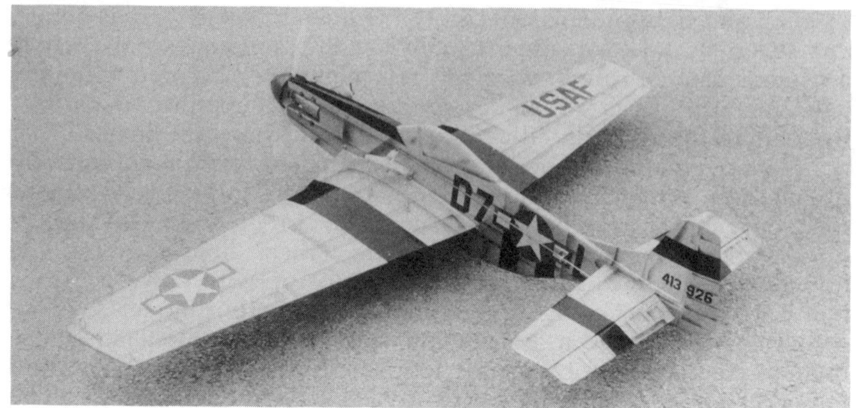
A profile fuselage need not mean an ugly model. Skilful spray-painting of panel lines, insignia and markings makes this profile P-51 Mustang an attractive and instantly recognisable aircraft.

Team racing involves three models racing simultaneously, which requires concentration to avoid line tangles. Engine size and fuel capacity are limited, making pit stops for refuelling necessary, and each team has a mechanic to cope with this. Catching the model, refuelling and restarting can take as little as 7-8 seconds with a good team. There are variations – rat-racing, Goodyear, etc. – but these relate to model specifications and the general conduct of a race remains similar.

Combat is an exciting event where normally two but sometimes three models are flown together, each trailing a long tissue streamer. The aim is to cut pieces off the opposing streamers, scoring points for each cut, while avoiding one's own streamer being cut. The models are fast, light and highly manoeuvrable and, as may be imagined, need to be easy to repair.

Because the lines stabilise the models in roll and a small amount of engine and/or rudder offset will keep the lines taut, leaving only free movement in pitch, many models can be flown on control lines which would not otherwise be sufficiently stable or suitable for free flight and might be marginal under radio control, even in the hands of an expert flier. A lot of scale models which would be dubious flown free are quite docile on control lines, and there are builders who put so much work into a model that they are unwilling to risk damage by, perhaps, flying in strong winds under radio. There is thus a strong interest in scale c/l models and some truly magnificent models are seen.

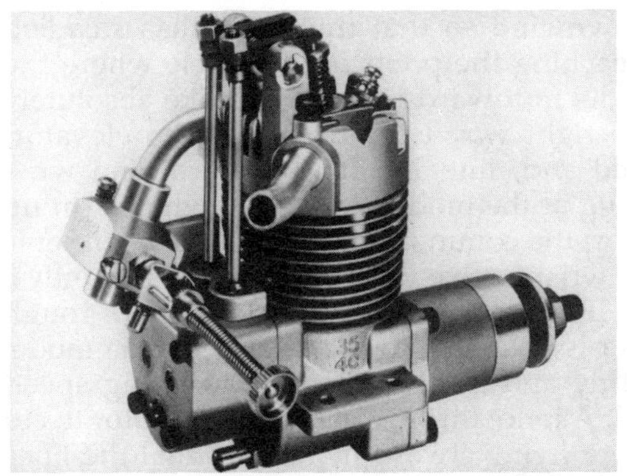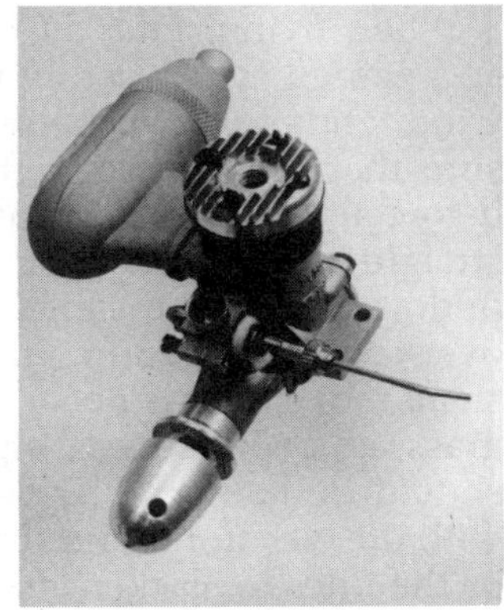

Four-stroke glowplug engines are increasingly popular, for scale models, radio or control-line, in particular. Japanese 6cc example, left. A German 1½cc two-stroke (minus glowplug) is compared on the right.

One other type of competition is worth mentioning, the carrier event. Here models are taken off and landed on a low platform representing an aircraft carrier deck, curved to fit the circle, and are awarded points for the differential between maximum speed and the slowest at which they can be flown and controlled.

First Steps

Control-line flying has the advantages that it needs a relatively small space, gives the modeller direct control over his model and enables him to choose models which would not be totally airworthy in other formats. The disadvantage is that the engine runs throughout the flight and is thus a continual noise which non-modellers find irritating. It may be possible to fly on a recreation ground surrounded by houses, but from a public relations viewpoint it is not perhaps desirable.

A beginner should choose a simple, rugged trainer, probably of all-sheet construction and possibly with a profile fuselage. The bigger the engine/model the easier it is to fly, as a general rule, especially as longer lines can be used. Propellers are usually of coarser pitch than for free flight, because the model flies faster, and a control-line fuel tank should be used, feeding from the outer side of the tank, where the fuel will be flung by centrifugal force. The most important points in building are a strong anchorage for the bell-crank pivot and completely free movement of the elevators and linkage – the elevators should drop under their own weight if the model is turned over.

When flying, take off downwind so that the model has steadied and gained speed before reaching the point on the circle where the wind tends to blow the model in towards the pilot. Make absolutely sure that the handle is the right way up ("up" gives up elevator) before the model is released and, initially, hold the arm and wrist straight and stiff and pointing at the model. Move the whole arm up or down to move the elevator; the commonest fault with a beginner is over-control by bending the wrist to give full up or down when only a small movement is needed. If take-off is impossible because of rough grass, an experienced helper is desirable to hand-launch. The model should be launched smoothly and level at or close to flying speed with the elevators at neutral. A jerky throw can cause the motor to cut or the lines to slacken. Before flying always make sure that the lines and connections are in good condition and that the flying circle is clear.

Radio control

Radio flying constitutes the major part of organised aeromodelling nowadays, insofar as it has the biggest following in most clubs and, in fact, many clubs are radio-only. The model trade is also largely geared to radio control, to the extent that apart from a few f/f and c/l kits and engines, only enthusiast model shops offer many of the smaller bits and pieces for non-radio models.

Modern R/C equipment is of the instal-and-switch-on type, needing no specialised radio knowledge, and provided batteries are in good condition and regular simple maintenance is carried out, it is totally reliable. In the early days there was a great deal of single-channel (rudder only) flying, but today most basic sets provide two functions (usually used for rudder and throttle or rudder and elevators, sometimes ailerons and elevators) although only one need be used, of course; small models and vintage aircraft may well have rudder control only, used to steer the model to prevent it flying away rather than to alter its flight pattern. This may be termed "radio assist".

Other equipment offers three, four, six or even seven functions. Four would be used as a rule for rudder, elevator, ailerons and throttle, and additional functions for undercarriage retract, flaps and perhaps special effects. Advanced equipment can provide servo reversal, rate control, exponential control and programming. In the last you can set, say, a slow roll into the equipment and subsequently every time the roll button is pressed the aircraft will perform a slow roll. Rate control allows control sensitivity to be reduced for high speed flight, while exponential control varies sensitivity over the range of control stick movement, giving more precise control where it is important.

A fully aerobatic model can perform any of the manoeuvres of full-size aerobatic machines and takes considerable skill and practice to fly well. Learning to fly a radio model is safest if instruction is given by an experienced pilot who can take over if the learner becomes confused; "buddy box" equipment is available which allows the instructor's transmitter to be linked to the pupil's so that he can immediately take over to get the model out of an awkward position. Those who must learn alone are advised to start with a powered glider or a slow-flying trainer where situations develop less suddenly and give the learner a little more time to register and react. The commonest problem is over-correction, often arising from the slight delay in the response of the model to initial small corrections.

Sport models may lie anywhere between rudder-only and rudder/throttle/elevator/ailerons and much of the pleasure comes from flying smoothly and, particularly, making a good approach and landing. Aerobatics may be confined to loops and rolls with perhaps an

Large-scale models have become firmly established over the last three or four years, but need experience in building and flying, as well as a special Permit to Fly. This Ju87 *Stuka* is a fine example.

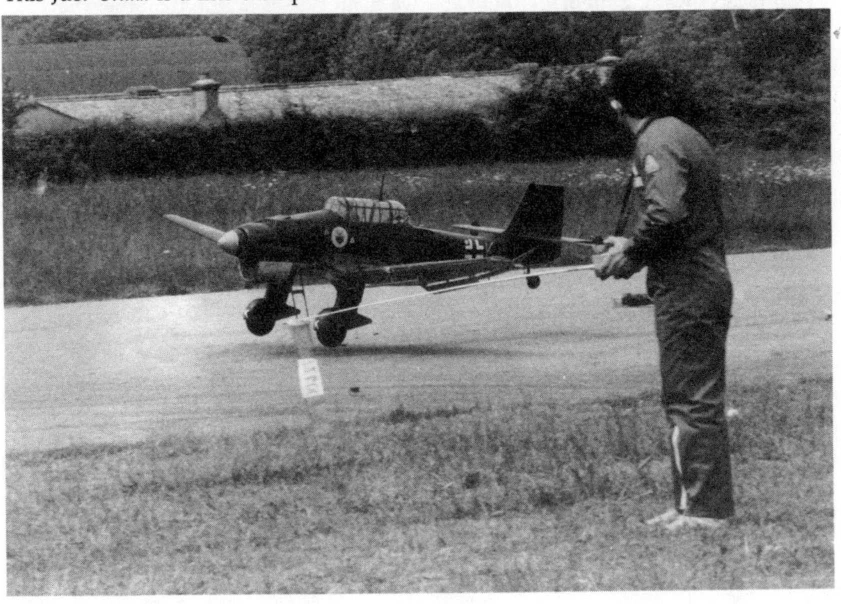

occasional stall turn or roll-off-the-top. More advanced models and equipment will be used by those prepared to practise and polish manoeuvres with a view to competition flying.

One specialist R/C field is pylon racing, where four or five highly tuned models take off simultaneously and race for a number of laps round a triangular course marked by pylons. Marshalls observe that each model passes outside each pylon and speeds are in the order of 200 k.p.h. plus.

Over the last few years, scale models have come to dominate R/C flying. In skilled hands, almost any full-size aircraft can be flown in scaled-down form with the aid of radio control and the range of models seen at large meetings extends from the very early days of powered flight to the latest jets. The latter use a powerful and high-revving engine to drive a fan inside a duct and many years of development have led to sufficient thrust to fly accurate scale models at realistic jet-like speeds. The popular era is, however, World War 2, with the Spitfire and the Mustang vying for the position of most-modelled aircraft. Multi-engined machines are not uncommon and there are floatplanes, flying boats and amphibians and every variety of aircraft you can think of. There are special events for scale Schneider Trophy seaplanes, for example.

Pylon racers awaiting the flag. There are two main classes and in the other the models must take off the ground. Hard hats are customary – these models fly at some 130 m.p.h.

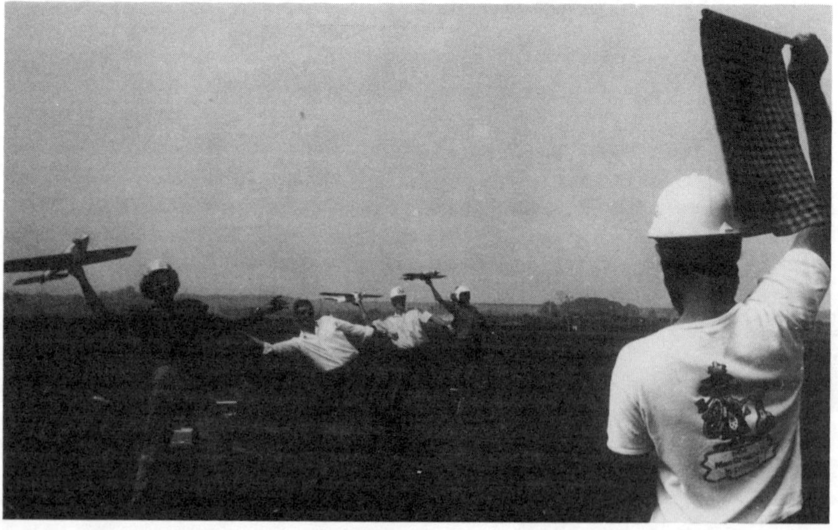

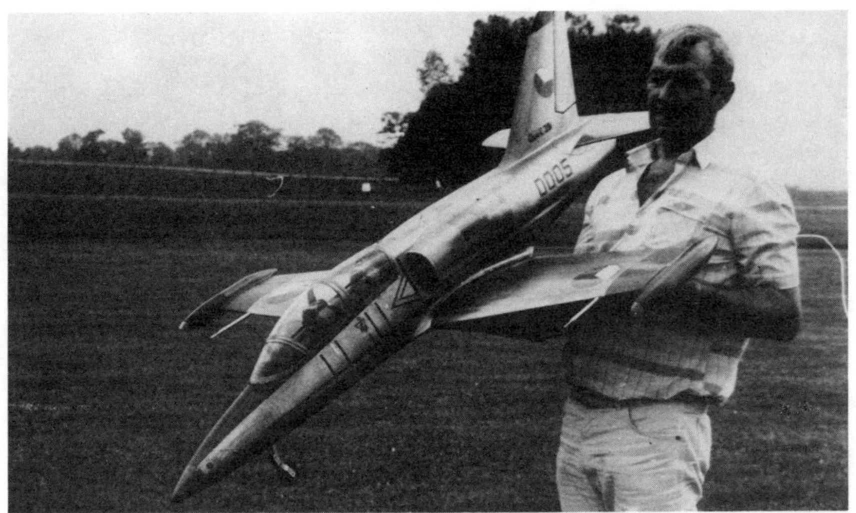

A splendid example of a ducted fan model, this Aero L39 *Albatros* uses a 10cc engine and a commercial fan unit and performs just like the prototype. Not a project for an absolute beginner.

It has always been acknowledged that the larger a model is, the easier it is to fly, and this applies particularly to radio, especially to multi-engined models. Early scale radio models of, say, a single-engined fighter were often ⅛ or 1/7 of full-size, but in the search for better flying and more fine detail the scale rose to 1/6 or 1/5. This increase has led, in the last few years, to Large Scale Models, ¼, ⅓ and even ½ full size for small prototypes. Such models exceed the 5Kg. weight limit accepted for models internationally and need a special Permit to Fly; they also need careful structural design and meticulous construction and are not for the average beginner! The largest so far is probably a 20 ft. Lancaster model, flown regularly at demonstrations.

Gliders

The difference between gliders and sailplanes used to be that the latter had soaring ability, i.e. it could climb above its launch point, whereas a glider made a continual descent. Nowadays the terms are effectively interchangeable. Even when soaring a glider or sailplane is continually descending, but if it gains height the air through which it is flying is obviously rising faster than the machine's rate of descent.

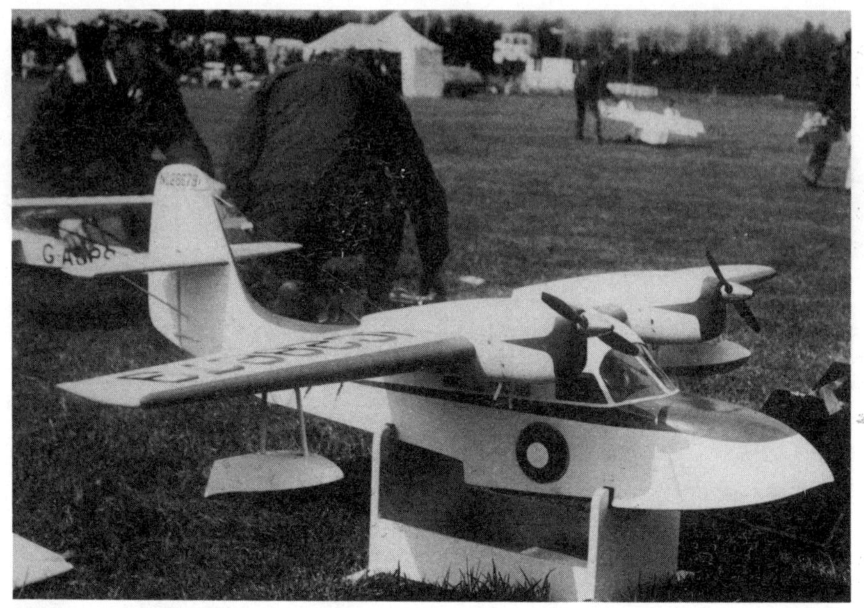

Interest has been growing in waterplanes. This Grumman *Gosling* has the best of both worlds, able to fly off water or, as in this picture at Old Warden aerodrome, equally happy on grass.

Rising air is generally referred to as "lift" and corresponding descending air as "sink".

Wind blowing over the ground is deflected upward when it comes to a hill and, depending on the windspeed and height and angle of slope a band of lift will extend out from the slope face. This slope lift will persist while the wind direction and speed remain roughly constant and if its vertical component exceeds the sinking speed of a glider, the machine can remain aloft for hours on end. This is slope soaring.

Lift is also – and more widely – created by temperature differences in air, warmer air rising as a thermal current under the normal principles of convection. The sun passes through air without warming it, but it heats the ground etc. and this in turn warms the air by conduction. Air over, say, a road will be warmed more than that over an adjacent field and when the temperature difference is sufficient, or a disturbance takes place, the warmer air will break away as a thermal bubble. Exploiting this continual process is called thermal soaring, or sometimes, for R/C gliders, "flat field flying".

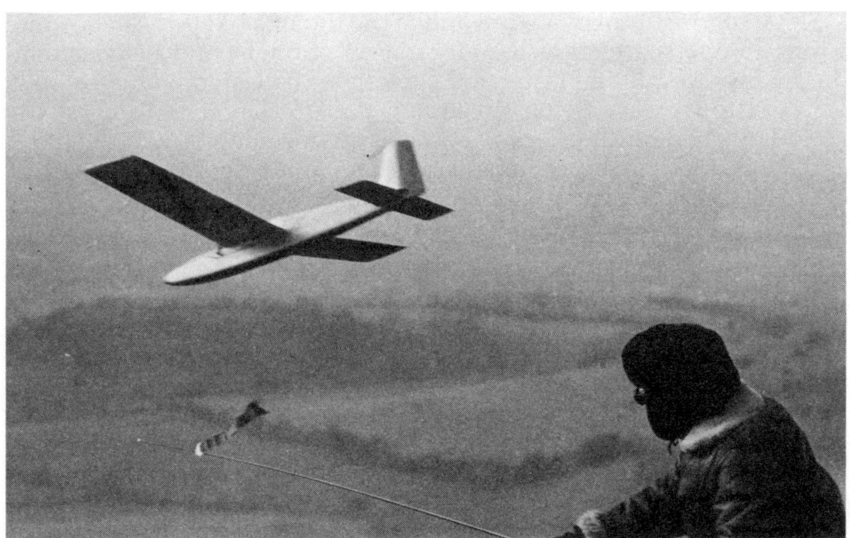

Above, a fairly hefty heave is needed to launch a slope-soarer. This is the sort of model a beginner could well consider.

Below, the wings flex under the strain as this towline scale-type glider noses into a fast climb. Note parachute on line end.

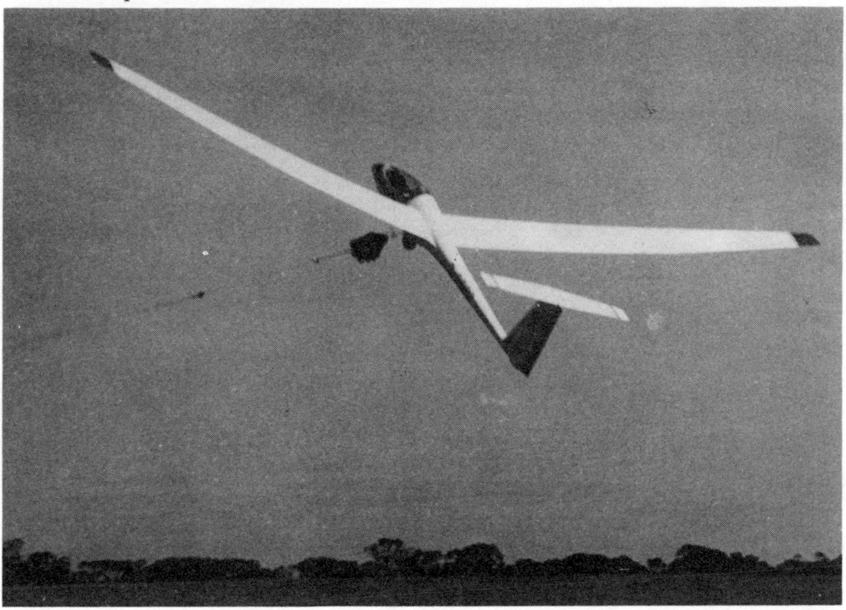

Slope soaring implies a wind and at the top of a hill this can be quite strong. Slope soarers are therefore often stronger and heavier than thermal soarers, flying faster and sometimes ballasted with steel rods or water to increase flying speed and penetration. They are usually hand-launched off the slopes. Thermal models may be a little lighter and larger, perhaps aiming for a more floaty flight, although in competitions these may also be ballasted. Although they may be towed up by a power model, the normal methods of launch are by towline or bungee. Towing may be by a hand winch plus some running by the tower, or by a power winch using an electric motor and a car battery. One technique is to winch the model up very fast, almost catapulting it off the top of the launch and using the excess speed to gain extra height; this calls for strong wings. A bungee launch uses a stretchable section (usually surgical tubing) of about a quarter of the towline length, the model being taken back to stretch the line before release. This too needs adequate wing strength.

Gliders tend to sound big. Although there are 2 metres and

Aero-towing gliders is not a means of launching for 'official' competitions but is great fun. As one pair settle in the air a second tug prepares to take off, the glider being hand-launched at matching speed.

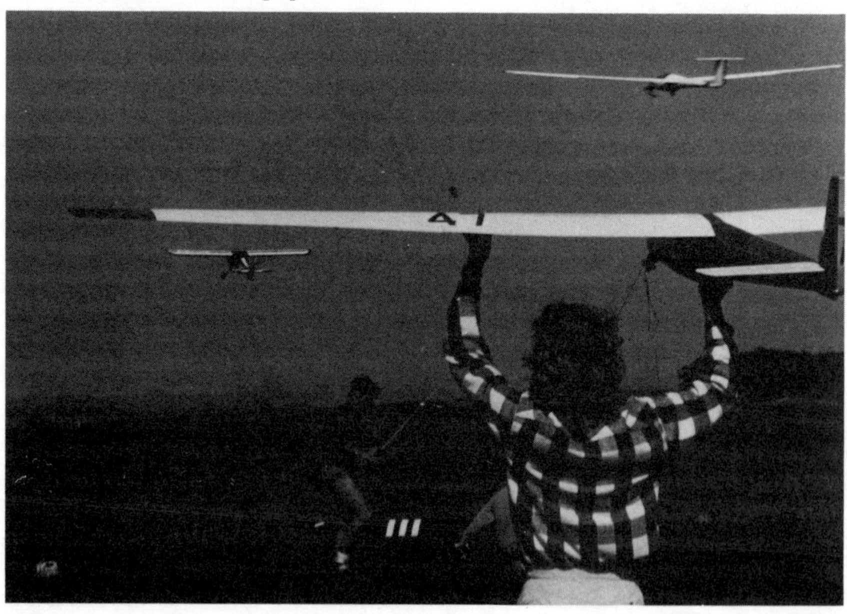

100 inch classes, many models are 10, 12 even 16 ft. and more in span, but because they use high aspect ratios (long, narrow wings) the actual wing area of, say, a 16 ft. model may be about the same as that of a 6-7 ft. power model.

Keeping a model airborne in slope lift is not difficult in a suitable wind, though it requires skill in marginal conditions. Long flights with a thermal soarer, however, mean knowing where to look for lift and making the best use of it when found. Good slope lift enables an aerobatic glider to be put through its paces and provides the opportunity to fly engineless scale jet fighters at high speeds in a surprisingly realistic way.

Scale models of full-size sailplanes are well established and fly well. Many prototypes fit the 15m. category and 1/5 models of them are therefore all about 10 ft. span. Probably at present a majority of scale types are flown on slopes rather than from the flat.

Competitions often include three or more tasks, which may be a minimum or specific duration, speed round a triangular or two-point course, cross-country courses with fixed turning points, spot landings and so on. Distance flying, by a team using a small pick-up truck to follow the model, is a challenge which appeals to some fliers. In good conditions a team of driver, navigator, spotter and pilot can find a flight of 100 miles or so a tough but exciting undertaking.

Single-handed flat field fliers may resort to a small pod-mounted engine to take the model up to a reasonable height. A development is electric power, where a two-minute run might take the model to 5-600 ft., when the motor is switched off by radio. If lift is scarce and the model nears the ground a further power run is possible to regain height, after which there should be enough power left to position the model for landing, if necessary. With quick-charge nicads a 15 min. charge enables a further flight to be made; a minimum flight time should be 12-15 mins. but if lift is about it can be much longer. Electric power can be used in aerobatic models and even in some scale aircraft, but its commonest use is in glider types.

Helicopters

Although both rubber and power helicopters have occasionally appeared in free flight form, this type of aircraft did not achieve popularity until the advent of radio control and the development of the engineering aspect to a point where kits could be offered. The complexities of the rotor drive and control system call for considerable design and engineering skills and the practice is to provide this part of a model ready-made and, usually, ready assembled in kit form models which follow scale appearance quite closely.

Flying a helicopter has been compared to balancing a steel ball on a knife-edge while riding a bicycle. It is not an easy art to learn, but the fact that hundreds have managed it indicates that with patience it can be done. The models behave just like full-size machines, or perhaps take performance further, since a top pilot can fly a model inverted, which is not often seen in full-size! Learning to fly one usually starts with a tethered model which lessens the risk of a severe crash and, if a short enough tether is used, should reduce rotor breakage. Once the learner can keep the model in a steady hover position the tether can be lengthened to allow very gentle exploration of movement, always returning to a static hover. Untethered, very tiny control movements can be tried, and so on. Possibly 6-8 hours of flying will be needed before full flight is attempted.

Materials and flying

Radio models have seen the introduction of many new materials to construction, including foam wings, g.r.p. fuselages and heat-shrink covering, but it is still possible to build and fly successful models using balsa, ply and tissue or nylon covering. Traditional materials do, in fact, produce an airframe which is easier to repair than one built of more "modern" substitutes, and this is a point worth considering by a beginner. Few people become competent model pilots without occasional damage to a model.

Seek advice to choose a proved beginners' model and follow the designer's intentions throughout. No doubt you can recognise obvious points of stress, but avoid the temptation to add your idea of reinforcement and trust the designer. Beefing up the structure adds weight, increasing flying speed and thus stresses, requiring more reinforcement – the usual spiral with model aircraft. The designers' experience has shown him what structure is needed to combine adequate strength with reasonable flight performance.

Expanded polystyrene (foam) is insufficiently strong of itself for wings etc. and is most often supplied ready veneered, the veneer providing the strength and rigidity needed. The foam is also attacked by many adhesives and paints, and instructions should be followed faithfully. Wing panels are usually joined by cloth tape and polyester resin applied externally. An advantage of ready-made foam wings is that they are likely to be true; accidental warps are a major cause of flying difficulties.

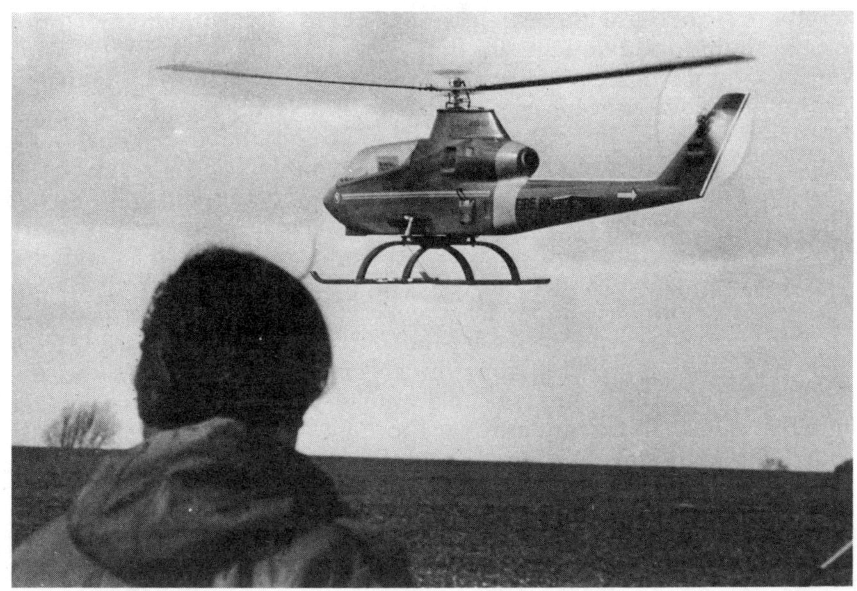

One of the model helicopter pioneers, Dieter Schluter, flying his Bell *Huey Cobra*. Because of the engineering content, helicopters tend to be costlier than other models, as well as harder to fly!

A very important contribution to flight success is correct positioning of the model's centre of gravity or, in practice, making sure that it balances in accordance with the instructions. Slight nose-heaviness may be acceptable but on no account try to fly a model which balances behind the recommended point. Correct balance, freedom from unintentional warps, accurate alignment of flying surfaces and a thoroughly checked radio giving correctly-sensed free-moving but rattle-free controls are four major points essential for trouble-free flight performance.

Engines

The glowplug type of engine is by far the most used in model aircraft. It relies for ignition on a tiny wire coil in the plug which glows when heated by a 1.5 or 2 volt battery, connected for starting purposes. Once running a combination of combustion heat and catalytic action between coil and fuel gases keeps the plug glowing and the battery can be disconnected. The fuel used is basically methyl alcohol (methanol) and oil with, usually, an addition of nitro-methane and it has a slight disadvantage in that it attacks many paint or dope finishes, so that special paints or a fuel-proof varnish must be used.

These engines can be less than half of 1cc. up to, in two-stroke form, 10 or 15cc. In recent years four-strokes have become more popular, especially for scale and large scale models and vintage types, due to some extent to lower noise output and the ability to swing large propellers at useful power levels. Early four-strokes were always spark-ignition with a battery, coil and condenser or a magneto, but modern versions use glow ignition. Sizes range from 3½ to 20-30cc. or, in multi-cylinder form, even larger. Many enthusiasts use electric starters to avoid propeller-flicking, and it is even possible to fit self-contained on-board starters on larger models.

Diesels, so-called, are still extremely widely used on smaller models, especially but not only for sport use. The size range is usually .5 to 3.5cc. although 5cc. is not unknown. Fuel is commonly paraffin, oil and ether, often in approximately equal parts, and ignition is simply a result of the heat generated by high compression.

Pulse jets were used for control-line speed models 35 years ago but are rarely used today because of insurance difficulties, although one Dutch team provides spectacular 300 k.p.h. plus demonstrations with R/C deltas powered by this type of engine. Recently a British experimenter has achieved success with a miniature gas turbine jet, but at present virtually all jet models employ the ducted fan.

Beginners

The easiest introduction to model flying, either free flight or radio, is a glider, but not too small a one. There are many suitable kits and plans for first models. More can be learned with a rubber-powered model for those with the time and patience, but again it should not be too small – about 30 ins. span is reasonable. Otherwise a small-engined free-flight model, or a power-assisted glider for radio, could be a starting point. Something simple, rugged and fairly slow flying should be the aim, and this applies equally to a first model for someone interested in C/L flying. As has been repeated throughout this book, joining a club is the best and quickest way to learn, but if this is not possible, take comfort in the thought that thousands have become competent modellers through their own efforts. Read everything you can find and use patience, care and common sense and you will soon be sharing the pleasures enjoyed by everyone who persevered through the early stages.

Model Railways 5

There are more people attracted to model railways as a hobby than any other form of modelling, but there are two major differences which put railways in a category of their own. One is total independence of weather and the other the fact that more than 90% of practitioners buy all their requirements readymade; in the case of locomotives and rolling stock the percentage is higher and the modern acronym is "RTR" – ready to run. The vast majority of railway modellers may lay track and construct scenic accessories but are content to operate with commercially-produced engines, coaches and wagons.

This is not the impression one receives from model railway exhibitions, but these are staged by enthusiasts, some of whom have the skill and experience to build a locomotive kit or, as commonly

The differences in size between (from the rear) 0, 00, N and Z gauges is graphically demonstrated in this picture.

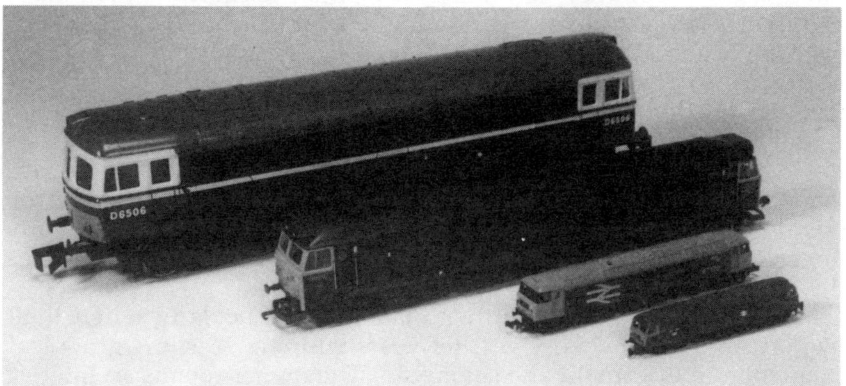

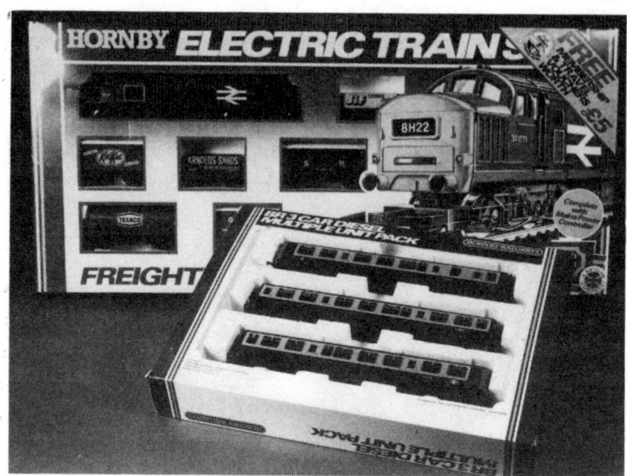

Most people start with a boxed set like these; stage 2 is to build one's own permanent track layout.

occurs, to modify a commercial model. A high proportion of club members are prepared to make their own wagons and coaches, from kits or available parts, and some will make their own track, but the standard of present-day commercial products is so high that it is difficult for an average modeller to equal them, let alone improve on them. What tends to happen is that stock is "personalised" by modification or repainting to represent a specific prototype, or simply "weathered" to give a truer representation of working equipment, and the modeller concentrates on producing as convincing and realistic a layout as possible.

In the same way, model railway magazines tend to give a rather specialised picture of the hobby, with much of their content providing interest and inspiration to readers who wish to improve their skills and their railways, but at the same time a lot of what is published is over the heads of the mass of model railway customers. The average newcomer to model railways buys a boxed set, plugs the oval of track together on the floor or on a table and quite happily runs his train round and round. He may well progress to one or two sidings, with manually-operated points, in which case the track may be permanently set out on a baseboard, but because of lack of space the board may have to be stored on edge or slid under a bed, so that any degree of scenic work becomes impractical and imagination provides the environment when the layout is in operation.

Many railways get no further than this, particularly when their owners are youngsters. Over the years running sessions grow less frequent and eventually the set is sold. The owner retains an interest

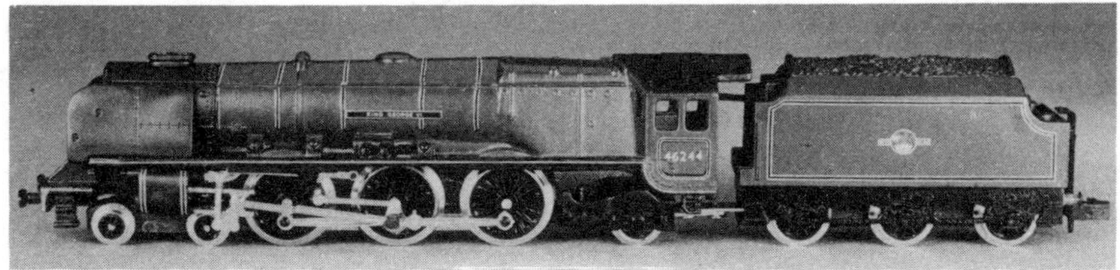
RTR locomotives in 00 gauge are of high standard . . .

but ceases to be active until, perhaps, he has a house of his own or sons of his own. There is, however, a great deal more to model railways than this and an enthusiast will always feel rather sad that our typical newcomer did not progress sufficiently far to encounter the real challenges and rewards of the hobby. Nevertheless, this basic approach to model railways obtains in the majority of cases and creates a market providing the greater part of the turnover in the

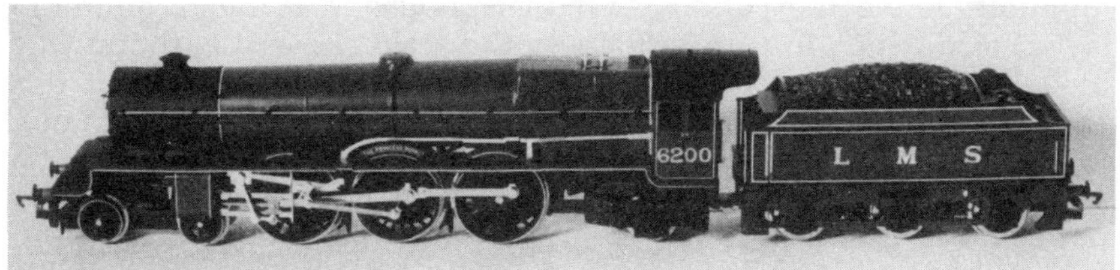
. . . even compared with nicely-built kit examples . . .

model railway trade: without such a mass market there would be fewer sources of supply and less commercial experimentation and development, which would mean a more limited choice.

At the other end of the scale, there are very few experts able to build, say, a complete locomotive from raw materials. Most will buy ready-cast wheels or finished motors, the latter possibly spares from commercial engines or adaptations of motors originally produced for,

. . . or scratch-built engines by expert modellers.

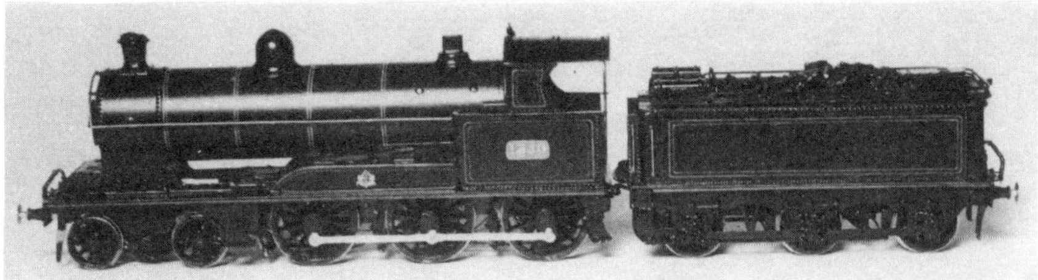

perhaps, instrument work. Cast and turned wheels, wagon solebars and axleboxes, strapping, coach chassis and many other components which are casting or capstan lathe products are usually offered by small specialist firms, often one or two-man businesses, supplying by mail order or through retail suppliers catering for enthusiasts. Some of these firms supply complete kits for locomotives, in plastic, die-cast white metal, or stamped or etched brass or nickel silver, either with chassis or to fit an available chassis. A wide range of kits for coaches and wagons can be bought, as can drawn rail for those who want to make the track itself, plus chairs, frogs and bits and pieces of every description.

Size

Most model railways are built and operated indoors (hence the immunity to weather) and with modern houses this means a limit to layout size which in turn influences the scale chosen. Early railway models were to no particular scale and few ran on track, but this changed at the turn of the century when manufacturers in Germany, England and America settled on 0 gauge, using 32mm. track and a scale of approximately 7mm. to 1ft., which remained the most popular size until the 1930s.

Initially, commercial products found a market with enthusiasts and sons of the relatively well-off, but as people became more mechanically-minded demand grew. The best-known name in model railway history is undoubtedly Frank Hornby, who introduced Hornby Trains in 1920 and to a great extent met the demand for

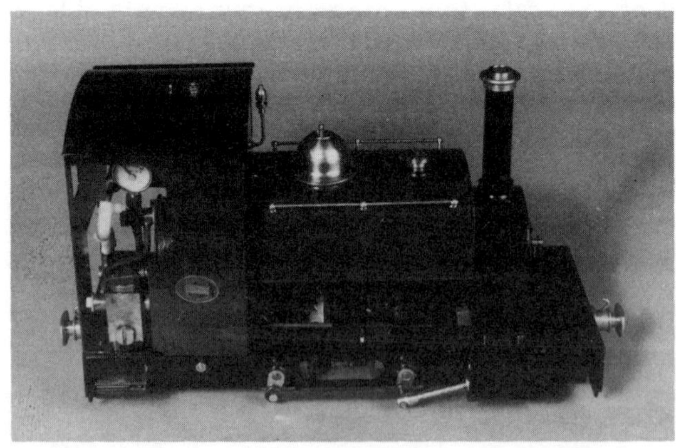

Live steam models in 1 or sometimes 0 gauge, intended for garden railways, can still be found. Some builders even make then in 00 gauge.

76

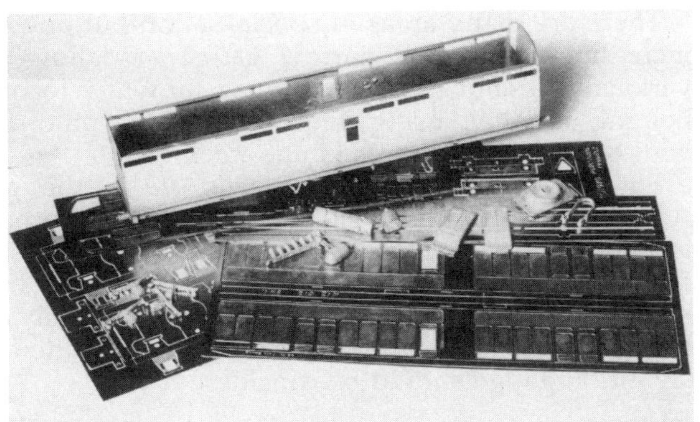

comparatively low-priced railway models of a good standard. Enthusiasts were catered for by several specialist firms, but to the average man "Hornby" was synonymous with model railways.

An 0 gauge layout required a fair amount of space, however, and a number of enthusiasts built half-size, or 00 models, at 3½mm. to 1 ft. Early commercial ventures in this size were unsuccessful, but in 1938 Hornby introduced 'Dublo' sets. It had been found that 3½mm. scale on 16.5mm. track was rather too small for the electric motors of the day to be fitted in British-outline locomotives, but 4mm. scale, also on 16.5mm. track, gave sufficient room. This was the approach followed by Hornby and the new scale achieved instant success. An 0 gauge layout could be reproduced in 00 gauge in a quarter of the space, an important consideration for the majority of potential customers.

The larger prototype Continental locomotives enabled one or two European manufacturers to proceed with 3½mm. scale, which became known as H0 to differentiate between the rolling stock although the same basic track size was used. At 4mm. scale the track gauge should be 18.8mm.; there are specialist groups who employ this gauge and others who use 18.0mm., but the inaccuracy of scale resulting from running 4mm. trains on 16.5mm. track is not of major concern to the vast majority of its users and 00 has proved the most popular size in Britain.

Shortly after the establishment of smaller size railways came World War 2 and a general cessation of development and manufacture, but in the post-war years a number of even smaller introductions were made. TT gauge (3mm. on 12mm. track) had a brief commercial life, as did a Continental 2½mm. system. The most popular of the smaller scales has proved to be N gauge (2.06mm. on 9mm. track) although Z gauge (1½mm. on 6.5mm. track) is even smaller.

There are many areas of specialisation but one which is attracting increasing support is narrow gauge modelling. This is found in various scales but the most popular, for which locomotives etc. can be bought, is 00n9, using 4mm. scale for scenic details and vehicle bodies but running on ·N gauge track.

For most British-based railways, 00 is the general choice. In America and Europe, H0 is usual, and as more British-outline locomotives become available in this gauge, some incursion on the 00 scene in Britain may be expected. Since the same track gauge is used, requirements of space are similar. If space is really at a premium, or if the interest is in creating the scenic setting rather than just the track layout, N gauge should be considered.

Track plans

Running on a simple "oval" track as supplied with the average boxed train set is fine for a time, but most owners soon feel the need to introduce points, sidings, cross-overs and other track extensions which enable more complex train operations to be practised. Study of various makers' catalogues, most of which include suggested layouts, is an enjoyable and instructive way of learning about possibilities and assessing what might be feasible in the space available.

A constraint with boxed sets is the use of constant radius curves and short straight lengths of track. Most makers offer alternative curves of different radii and various shorter sections of straight, permutations of which can be used to produce a varied track, but for realism it is necessary to obtain flexible track. A full-size railway line is characterised by long, gentle curves flowing from or into straight sections or bends of tighter radius. We have to accept that our track must have more frequent and sharper curves in order to fit into a reasonable space, and this in turn means that if a pair of lines is laid the space between them, the "six-foot" as it is known, has to be slightly wider than scale in order to allow clearance for the over-scale swing or throw of bogied rolling stock. Although this really applies only on curves, widening the space between lines only through curves looks worse than maintaining a constant over-width space, which tends not to be obtrusive. In 00 gauge, a space of 1⅜ in. (35mm.) between the inside rails will clear virtually all traffic, except perhaps on very sharp curves.

Many experts are content to have an end-to-end layout running along a shelf on one wall, or two walls, with perhaps a station at one end and sidings at the other. Obviously continuous (non-stop)

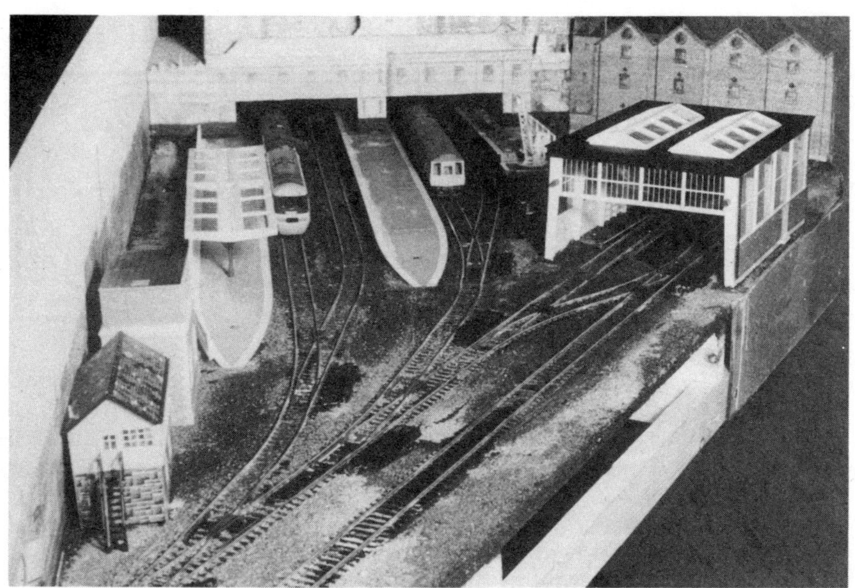

One way to embody a large station in a layout is to make half a terminus at one end of an end-to-end track. Extra width can be used to accommodate an engine shed, as in this Lowery layout.

running is not possible with such an arrangement, though some nice problems in train make-up can arise. The average enthusiast, however, is likely to want a continuous loop round which a train can run, even if only for a few laps at a time. Newcomers tend to think of main lines, but an eight-coach train plus locomotive would work out, in 00, at around 7 ft. 6 in. (2280mm.) long and main line terminus platforms would need to be twice this! For this reason most railway enthusiasts with a little experience think in terms of branch or suburban lines, with shorter trains and smaller, simpler stations and yards.

A continuous circuit needs a considerable width to accommodate a loop at either end and the average adult is likely to reach only about 3 ft. over a table-height surface. This would mean a fairly tight curve if the layout was against a wall or in a corner and the alternative is to make an aperture in the track base so that it is possible to duck under the base and stand in the aperture. Because most sheet materials are 4 ft. wide, this tends to be thought of as base width, allowing a 23 in. (585mm.) maximum radius, with an inner radius for a double line of 21 in. (534mm.), which is about a third of the smallest radius which could be used with any pretensions to exact scale.

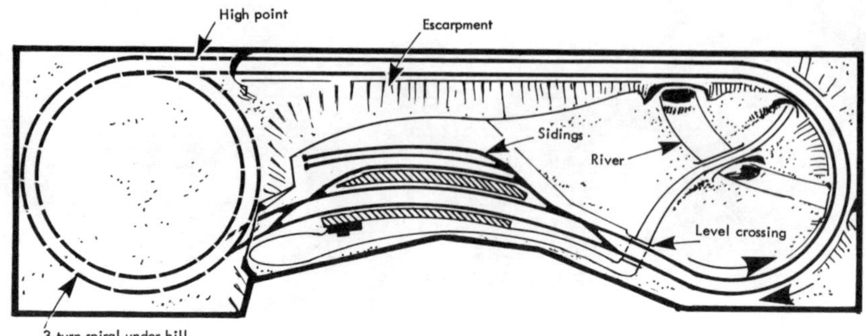

The maker's catalogue will give an indication of just how small a radius the train will negotiate but tight turns should be concealed behind or under scenery. A continuous track need not be parallel-sided but, if against a wall, may be an asymmetric dumb-bell with a narrow central section from which lines sweep out to the end curves. Sidings can be positioned in the area created by the outsweep of the main circuit, as shown in the diagram, which illustrates a general layout built twice in different scales by the author. The opportunity is offered by the hill to include a hidden spiral of track bringing the trains to a different height, allowing a long grade down to the opposite end. This provides plenty of scope for scenic work along the rear escarpment and on the hill, with perhaps a quarry or industrial area around the visible loop end, and so on. The length can be adjusted to suit the room, or the whole thing can be angled round a corner while still leaving usable space in the rest of the room.

One of the attractions of model railways is that you can give the imagination free rein. The basic layout shown can be altered, perhaps with the station on the graded part of the track, giving more room for sidings or perhaps a narrow gauge railway working a quarry. Point-work as drawn would make it simple to change train direction, increasing the interest in shunting manoeuvres, and so on.

Where a whole room is available an island site, with access from all sides, offers more scope, since there is more space to interlace two separate circuits and even to have different styles of station on opposite sides. With so many preserved lines nowadays it is even permissible to mix periods; one has only to think of, say, Blaenau Ffestiniog, where modern B.R. diesels pull in to one side of the new platforms and passengers cross to the century-old rolling stock of the narrow-gauge Ffestiniog waiting on the opposite side.

80

Baseboard construction

Most boxed sets are assembled on a carpeted floor and the mechanisms rapidly become choked with fluff. Operation on a table often means continual assembly and removal, which can lead to early electrical faults. Much more enjoyment, not to mentioned greater reliability, can be ensured by permanently mounting the railway on a baseboard. This may be a simple portable rectangle or one hinged to the wall or, in a garage, hoisted horizontally to the roof by ropes and pulleys, or it may be a semi-permanent structure built on trestles. In the last case a solid sheet of material is not needed and open-topped construction may be used.

A baseboard needs to be stiff and warp-free. Ply, blockboard or chipboard ⅜ to ½ in. (9-12mm.) thick can be used, whichever is cheapest, glued and screwed to a batten frame, with cross-battens every couple of feet or so. It should be possible to pick it up without it sagging or twisting, particularly if it is to remain portable. For more permanent location, it may be better to make it in two or more sections bolted together, which should be stiffer but, separated, easier to handle and making removal to a new home somewhat

Chipboard is used for the baseboard sections on this layout, which incorporates a figure 8 inside (at the far end, beyond) a basic loop. Polystyrene blocks form cutting walls etc. Clever design by David Lowery.

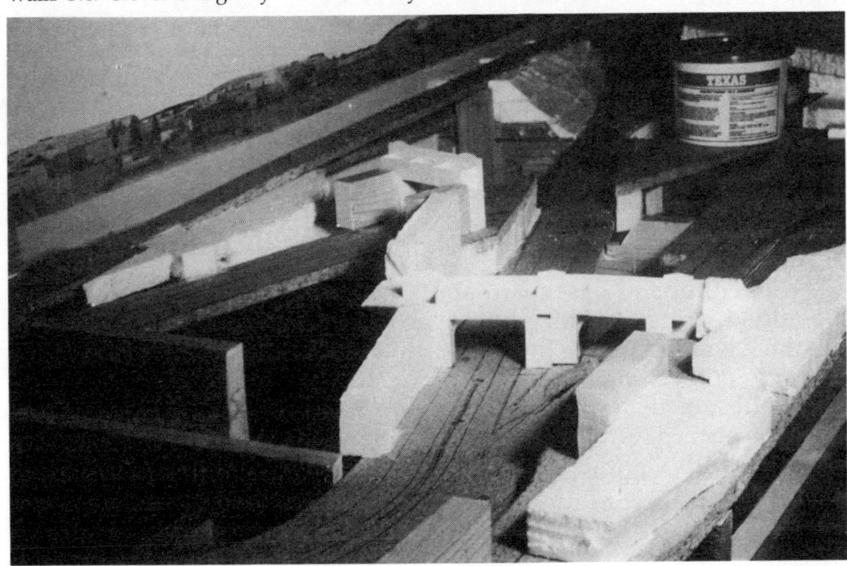

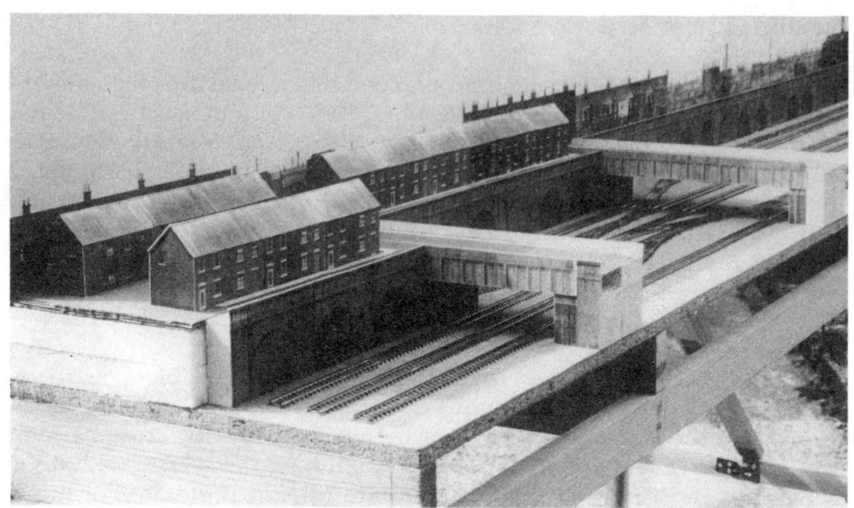

Track laid on underlay strip and ready for wiring. Notice the sturdy underframe and thick chipboard baseboard. Use of flat scenic background mixed with low relief and full structures produces excellent effect.

simpler if not too much major structural detail straddles the joint line. It also simplifies alteration or extension of the track should this arise in the future.

It is sometimes possible to acquire small chests of drawers or similar furniture at little or no expense; it is amazing what turns up at drive-in council waste disposal sites in the way of clean, usable furniture, for example. A baseboard set on a couple of chests can be made firm and the base then embodies considerable storage capacity. Otherwise stout legs should be glued and screwed firmly into corners of the frame. Height is very much an individual choice, experts suggesting 3 ft. to 3 ft. 6 in. (90-107cm.) but some people preferring normal table height.

An open-topped baseboard starts out as a braced frame to which are added strips of ½ in. ply etc. providing a solid base only where the track will run. Once these are screwed in place rigidity is assured. Changes of level can be introduced without difficulty and without the duplication of material incurred when a section is elevated above a solid baseboard. Areas to receive scenery on an open frame can be filled in with lighter material such as hardboard. For maximum economy the track plan can be laid out full-size on sheets of brown paper and the sections cut and positioned as templates on the ply or chipboard in such a way as to reduce wastage to a minimum.

Tracklaying

A common mistake with beginners is to lay the track directly on the baseboard instead of using an underlay. The recommended material is rubberised cork, available in 1 in. strips and stuck down with contact cement. Two strips side by side make a bed for a single line, but four are required for double lines. If the centre line for the track path has been drawn, a strip is stuck down aligned with this and the second strip butted to it. The third strip then automatically provides the centre line for the second pair of rails. Chamfer the outside edges of the strips with a sharp blade and, if desired, give them a coat of ballast-coloured paint before commencing to lay the track. The underlay not only gives the right basic shape for the ballast bed but makes running quieter and smoother.

Flexible track is supplied attached to sleepers and it is necessary to slide the sleepers along fractionally to achieve equal disposition when a curve is introduced. It is worth making up a little cutting block by sawing two grooves exactly at right-angles to the end face of a small

Convincing ballast adds to the realism of this picture and the less-than-new brickwork also contributes. Another David Lowery effort, photographed by Brian Monaghan, with excellent effect.

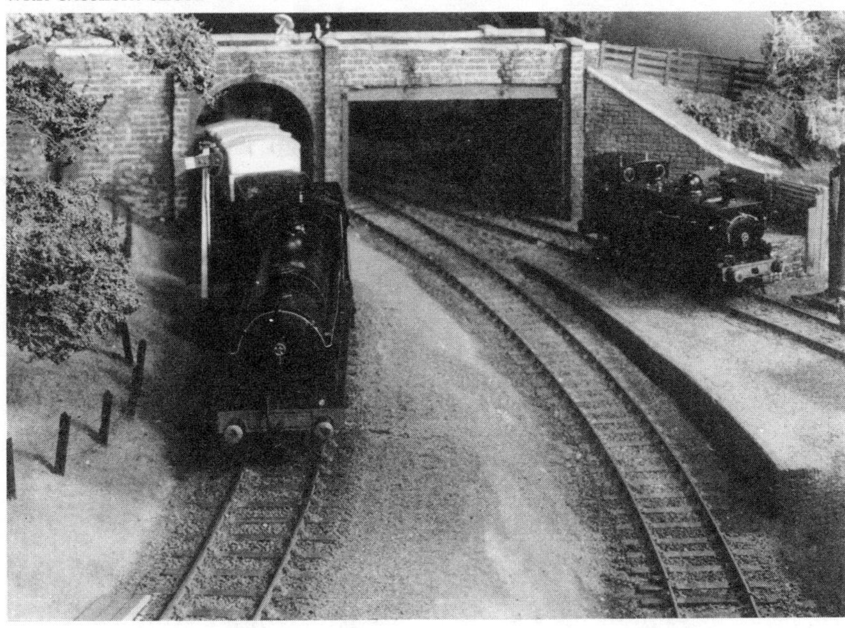

block of wood; the sawcuts, filed out as necessary, fit over the rails and hold them firmly while the end face provides a guide for a fine saw, enabling accurate square cuts to be made very simply. Joins are made by slipping fishplates on to the bottom flanges to hold the rail ends exactly aligned but free to slide a few thousandths of an inch if expansion or contraction occurs.

Start laying with the most complex piece, perhaps pointwork, and pin it temporarily in place. Add a length of track, sighting carefully for smooth curves and joints. Permanent pinning is not desirable as it can produce waves in the line, and white P.V.A. glue is recommended. If the track is lifted and the glue painted on the underlay, ballast can be scattered on. Crumbled (granulated) cork is sold for this but some builders employ dried used tea-leaves. P.V.A. dries clear and if the underlay was coloured beforehand a good result should be achieved without further painting, except for an all-over spray or large brush application of very thin dirty rust brown paint to take the newness off the track. Don't apply this until all soldered wiring connections have been made to the rails, and wipe off the top surface of the rails to leave them bright, both for appearance and electrical contact.

Wiring

Track wiring can get quite complicated with an elaborate layout but for a basic track it is straightforward. The usual simple system is a controller with a single knob, with current off in the centre position and increasing current in one direction or the other as the knob is turned, supplying the entire layout through feeds to two or three positions on the circuit, to avoid current drop through the rails. Such controllers are transformer/rectifiers plugged into the mains and supplying 12 volts D.C. to the track. If a double track main circuit is used and a train is to be run on each, a separate controller is needed for each track.

Normally joints in rails should be bridged by soldering a short wire linking the rails, about an inch from the end of each. Although metal fishplates will conduct current this is not their purpose and they cannot be relied on to continue to provide electrical continuity indefinitely. Sections of track can be isolated (so that one train can be stopped while another is manoeuvred elsewhere on the same circuit) by inserting plastic insulated rail connectors instead of metal fishplates at appropriate joints; the bridging wires are then extended to a switch, allowing the isolated section to be energised with the rest of

84

Microprocessors are
becoming standard
for control,
allowing several
chip-fitted loco-
motives to be run
on one track. Check
compatibility,
though, since
operating currents
etc, may differ.

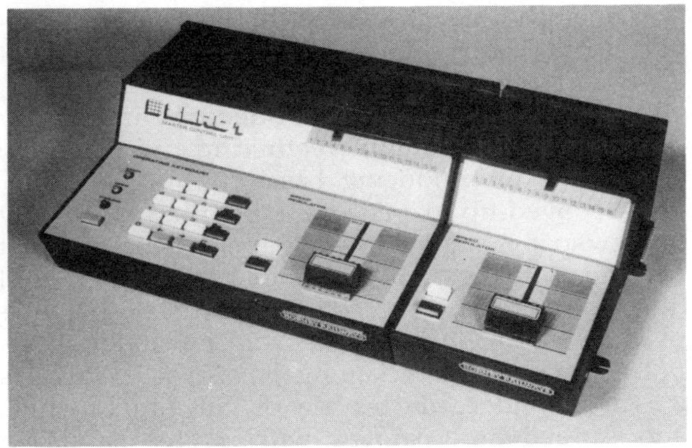

the line or switched out at will.

Most commercial turn-outs or points are designed so that when set for the main track the siding (etc.) is isolated, but many experts control shunting operations on a ladder of sidings with a third, independent controller, allowing the main up and down lines to keep trains running while shunting takes place. It depends on what the owner wants from his layout – the more ambitious his operations, the more complex the wiring. Most public libraries include examples of model railway books in which fuller details of wiring circuits can be found.

Scenery

To many enthusiasts model railways means trains moving through convincing surroundings and it is the construction of the track's environment that gives them an on-going interest. A look around a specialist model railway shop will show what a bewildering variety of scenic materials and ready-made accessories can be bought, but a layout does not have to be elaborate or have a great deal spent on it to look realistic.

Very few full-size railways run through totally flat country and making a flat layout look attractive is not easy. At the very least there should be some variation in contour, since a field painted flat on a smooth baseboard will never look realistic. The best course is to base a model on some nearby railway, where it is easy to pay occasional visits and sketch or photograph features which could be reproduced. The terrain should suit the railway – if you live in the fen country and are using, say, Caledonian stock the local landscape will be of limited use! A decision should also be made on the time of year and everything considered in accordance. Above all, however pleased you are with the neatness of buildings and so on, new, immaculate details rarely look right; weathering and wear must be represented.

Methods of producing basic contours include stout card boxes and screwed-up paper draped with four or five layers of torn-up newspaper soaked in wallpaper paste, wire netting crumpled and covered with hessian, subsequently painted with thin plaster, or other form of base covered with plaster cloth – the same as is used for plastering broken limbs, but sold in model shops. Scrap expanded polystyrene from packaging is also a useful basic material, since it is light and easily broken or cut and can be covered or carved and sanded and painted with poster paints for rock faces and the like.

Tunnels are always popular features and a wide choice of good portals can be bought, but it is necessary to have a hill at least three times the height of the tunnel entrance in order to justify the tunnel, and the line should approach the tunnel via a deepening cutting. Access to the line under the hill is necessary, for maintenance or correction of a derailment, and this can either be via an aperture cut in a vertical wall at the back of the hill or by making the hill above tunnel height removable. This might be achieved by fitting a batten frame to the baseboard to receive an insulation board "roof" plugging into it and cut to the general hill contour. The board edge can be chamfered and the hill constructed above and below the joint line, the chamfer forming part of the ground surface since, when hardened by painting with glue and paint, it will be less prone to damage than a plaster edge. A road, hedge, stand of trees, wall or combination of such details can be used to screen much of the joint.

Rock cuttings or faces can be made from expanded polystyrene, as mentioned, but tree bark is frequently used, especially that from the cork oak, or, for large areas, crumpled thick paper, which when worked on with paint, plaster, odd ferns etc. can be very satisfactory.

Natural growth

Growing plants are represented in a variety of ingenious ways, using dyed flock powders, sawdust, lichens and mosses and other unusual substances. A clever way to represent grass is to use green-dyed surgical lint pressed fluffy side down into wet plaster or glue; when dry the lint cloth is pulled away. Alternatively green flock powder can be scattered on wet plaster (mixed with green-dyed water) or P.V.A. glue painted on a surface. Hedges can be made from irregular lumps of synthetic sponge or coarse foam rubber, with a few small bits of plastic scouring pad interspersed, the whole painted brown or dark green at the base and lighter greens higher up, with different shades of flock powder scattered on the wet paint or, later, on wet glue brushed on. Variegation of colour and an absence of gloss are essential with all natural growth – indeed, with virtually all model railway scenery.

Trees can be bought, complete or in self-assembly form, but can often be improved by tearing them apart and reassembling in a less-formalised shape, painting the foliage dark beneath and lighter on top, scattering with flock powder and introducing colour variations and natural irregularities on trunk and branches. Quite reasonable trees can also be made from spiky twigs from bushes and plants, either wild or in the garden, painting appropriate areas with glue and rolling in crumbled foam, then painting and flocking. A bunch of lengths of florist's wire can be twisted, separated into branches, twisted some more, separated further and so on down to individual wires. The trunks and branches can be filled with plaster or car body filler, glue applied and tiny clippings of paper or natural seeds (such as birch) generously scattered several times, turning the tree each time. Such trees are better sprayed in greens, then the trunk and branches painted in various browns. Differing shades of green paper can be used to reduce the amount of spraying needed; complete fir trees can be made from dark green crepe papers by trapping a dozen or so cut-out profiles in a wire "hairpin", then opening out and ruffling the edges.

Buildings

Plastic card or balsa often forms the basis for buildings, which are then covered with brick and tile papers. Left at that the result is not very lifelike. There is a slight sheen on printed brick papers which should be deadened with matt varnish and some delicate dirtying of the brickwork in parts should be achieved, either by crayoning before varnishing or by occasionally touching the varnish brush lightly on some brushed-out brown/black paint. Scoring along the mortar lines also breaks the effect of flat, smooth surfaces. Roofs are better tiled with scored strips (paper for slates, postcard for flat tiles) overlapped and painted. Look at houses and other buildings to get chimney stack details, colour variations, gutter arrangements, lichen and moss

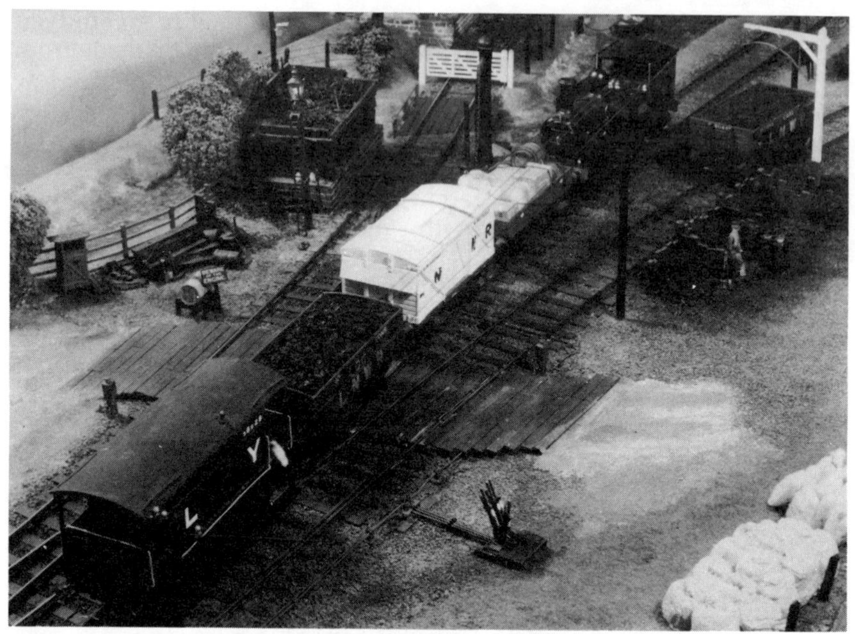

A splendid piece of scenic work, again by David Lowery, photographed by Brian Monaghan. Not only the liveries but the unattended tools (near the Lem Putt special on the left) are evocative of the 1920s.

growth etc., and note particularly that doors and windows are usually sunk into the wall, not flush with it.

For railway buildings and structures there is no shortage of illustrated books, but bear in mind the size of your layout. A reasonably accurate model of a small building is better than a severely compressed representation of something that is really much too long to fit in the space available. A common fault is the use of too thick or heavy materials for such things as glass canopies, fences, lamp posts and the like. It is useful to buy a couple of human figures in the appropriate scale and stand them near any item under construction to check proportions. Get into the habit of sizing things mentally – a 6 ft. square woven fence panel is just under an inch square in 00, under ½ in. square in N, a 9 in. diameter lamp standard is 3mm. or ⅛ in. in 00, 1½mm. or ¹⁄₁₆ in. in N, and so on. And look at your surroundings – is there any shine on a house other than window glass? What is the actual colour of a tarmac surface? How big are the slabs edging the platform at the local station? The more you observe, the more convincing your model will be.

Running

There are people whose pleasure comes mainly from operating their trains and to whom scenery is unnecessary. Working out marshalling moves on a network of track or interlinking train moves to a timetable is a source of satisfaction, and a little of this is desirable even for the scenic enthusiast. In either case a degree of maintenance will be inevitable.

Boxed sets plugged together for running and put away again are often set up on the floor; they frequently pick up a lot of carpet fluff and the continual making and breaking of the rail joints leads to deteriorating electrical contact. Gentle removal of fluff with a soft brush and, if necessary, a sharpened matchstick followed by the application of the merest trace of light oil to moving parts should be a regular job. Oil can be applied by means of a pin or the edge of a

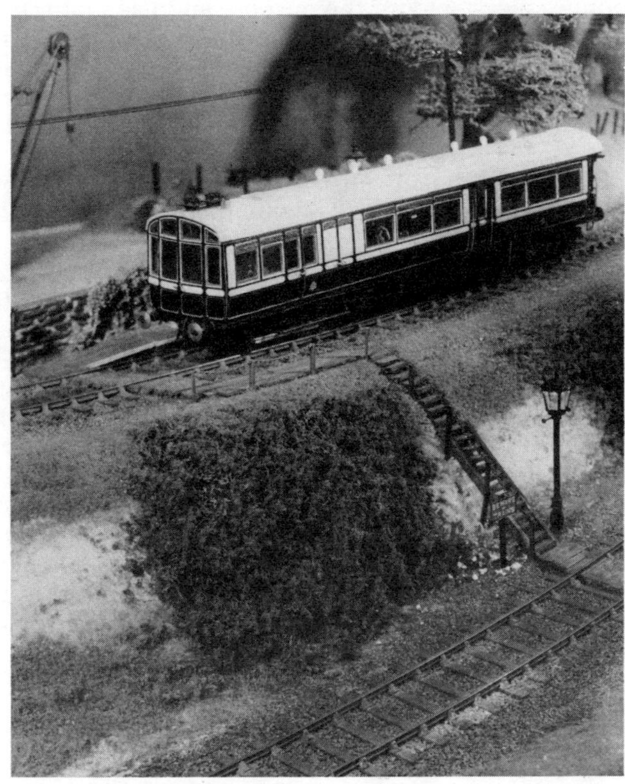

Another pastiche by the team opposite, a rail-motor stopped at a country halt. The track, the lamp-post, the wooden steps and the post-and-chain fencing are all absolutely right.

small, stiff feather. All rolling stock wheels should be checked for free rotation and couplings for correct operation.

Track joiners and rail ends should be cleaned occasionally with methylated spirit and the joiners checked for a reasonably firm fit. Packets of replacements are available at model shops.

Electrical continuity on these and permanent tracks can be checked with two wires and a bulb in the absence of a meter. Reduced or absent current can be isolated to a particular section and joints checked and renewed as needed. Soldered joints should give little trouble if competently made initially, but may require re-soldering. It is better to lift the track a little in order to clean the rails thoroughly to make a new joint; it will usually return to place without much sign of disturbance and a few minutes spent doing it properly will save future disappointment and frustration.

Rail tops and wheels gradually build up a patina which can interfere with current supply. Clean the rails with a rubber and pumice block sold for the purpose and use a slip cut from this to clean the wheel surfaces, especially the pick-up wheels. A glass-fibre or fine wire brush could also be used for wheels. Regular cleaning of track and wheels with a lint-free cloth damped with methylated spirit should avoid the need for an abrasive rubber but it is as well to have one for use on stubborn areas.

Follow the maker's instructions regarding locomotive maintenance, which will probably deal only with lubrication and commutator brush pressure. There is never any need to be brutal and it is a wise owner who seeks advice when in any doubt.

Model railway enthusiasts are fortunate in that there are probably more books on the subject than on any other field of modelling. It has only been possible to skim the surface of the subject in this chapter, but further reading on the whole subject, or particular aspects, is not difficult to find and the keen owner will read everything he can, visit exhibitions and model shops and if possible join a nearby club. Clubs are a source of advice, sometimes hard to get materials, and endless discussion on everything about railways; they provide encouragement and help and many build and operate layouts far more ambitious than the average individual could consider. As a member you become involved in such projects and have the opportunity of club visits to other clubs, outings to museums and workshops and many other activities.

Model Engineering 6

To many people, model engineering means simply live steam – locomotives, traction engines, marine and stationary engines all driven by steam – but it is really very much more than that. Probably "engineering on a small scale" is the closest encapsulation, because every process carried out in large-scale engineering is a part of model engineering, though there is one major difference. In normal engineering practice each aspect of a job is carried out by a specialist, a turner, a boilermaker, a grinder, a foundryman, a milling operator, a welder or whatever. A model engineer does everything himself, i.e. he has to have a working knowledge of just about every trade in engineering.

Obviously, a beginner is unlikely to have the breadth of experience necessary and he (sometimes she) will work from a published design, buying castings etc. and possibly enlisting the services of a pro-

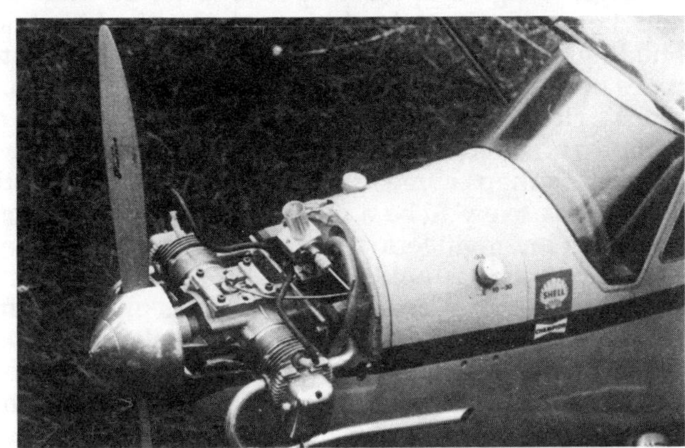

Combining aero-modelling with model engineering is a beautifully-made opposed twin engine in an equally well-built airframe.

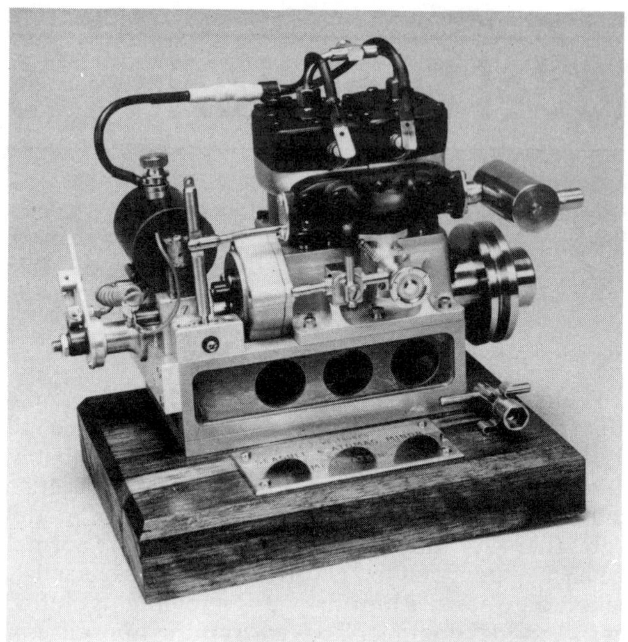

A two-cylinder in-line petrol engine suitable for marine use. Some builders even make their own sparking plugs.

fessional, or fellow club member, for perhaps brazing or welding or some other skilled job which he feels beyond his present capabilities. On the other hand, there are many model engineers able to design and draw up, say, a locomotive, make their own patterns and castings, design and make special tools, do their own blacksmithing and boiler work and all the other 101 skilled jobs necessary in building the model, even down to painting and lettering. With other types of model this might mean building a dynamo, making sparking plugs, clock cases, special burners, electric or electronic control equipment, special test rigs and virtually anything else.

It will perhaps come as no surprise to learn that the average model engineer is likely to be a mature man, frequently one who has spent his life in an engineering environment or whose daily work involves machinery. This is not to say that there are no young enthusiasts, for some schoolboys acquire the basic skills and interest at school metalwork classes or in their fathers' workshops. Similarly, an engineering backround is by no means essential since model engineers come from all walks of life: locally it is possible to think of a postman, a taxi-driver, a TV producer, a paper buyer, a dentist, a policeman, a plumber and others, besides several college lecturers and teachers and full-time engineers.

All these people have in common an insatiable mechanical curiosity and the desire to undertake precision work in metal. "Models" is something of a misnomer for what they produce, since they are miniature machines in their own right, built to a size which makes production in a small workshop feasible. Many are, of course, scale models of machines which do or did exist, but others are functional, original designs intended for working purposes. These may range from a petrol engine to propel a boat to a small air compressor and reservoir powering a hand-built spray gun; neither of these examples would be considered a difficult undertaking by the average enthusiast.

The Lathe

The basis of all model engineering work is the lathe, the "king of machine tools", which with a little ingenuity can be adapted to undertake virtually any machining job whatsoever. Compared with industrial production machines, our lathes are small and light and the rate of metal removal is relatively slow, but against that must be set the facts that our components are comparatively small and speed of work is not a vital consideration in a hobby. A single cleaning-up cut on an industrial milling machine could well remove half of a model component; if we are carrying out a milling operation on a lathe it doesn't matter if it takes half a dozen passes to achieve the right depth of cut provided the end result is what is wanted, and it hasn't been necessary to buy a milling machine.

Initial outlay for a lathe to set up a home workshop may seem considerable, though no more than might be spent on equipment by someone taking up golf or skiing, and a lathe will last a lifetime. There are other approaches: some modellers do not own a lathe but make use of one at an evening class or in a club workshop, doing all the hand work like setting out, sawing, filing and so on at home. More than one has built himself a lathe in this way. A common route is to buy a second-hand machine on which to learn the basics and simple lathes, old but in fair condition, can often be found for about one week's wages; a good machine capable of most model engineering work is likely to cost, second-hand, about four times this. In many clubs there are occasional sales of machines and tools surplus to members' requirements or being sold on behalf of a former member's estate. Often a member has an opportunity of buying quantities of surplus hand tools or materials and brings them along for clubmates to buy at, usually, bargain prices, with perhaps a small percentage of cash raised going to club funds.

Workspace has already been touched on in Chapter 1, but it is worth emphasising that a lathe properly mounted on a really solid floor will produce more accurate work more quietly than one stood on a suspended wooden floor, even if the joists are strutted beneath the machine site, as they would need to be. Solidity and weight are also important for a workbench, making work more enjoyable and accuracy easier, as anyone who has tried sawing or filing in a light vice clamped to a flimsy table will appreciate.

It would be fair to point out that forces are relative and that there are small table-top lathes which compare, in noise and forces involved, with a domestic electric sewing machine. Such little machines still benefit from a solid foundation, perhaps a heavy chest of drawers with all the tools and materials stored in the drawers to increase the weight. Inevitably a small machine imposes limits on the size of work possible, but this does not mean that "serious" model engineering cannot be carried out. Some surprising live steam and internal combustion engines have been made on baby lathes of 1¾ in. centre height, but the commonest size for model engineering is 3½ in.

Good quality tools kept sharp are essential for machine work, and this entails the possession of a bench grinder and an oilstone for honing. Also essential is a pillar drill of, usually, up to ⅜ in. (9mm.)

Steam road waggons went out of use around 50 years ago and are now occasionally seen at vintage rallies. They make splendid subjects for models, as evidenced by this one under construction.

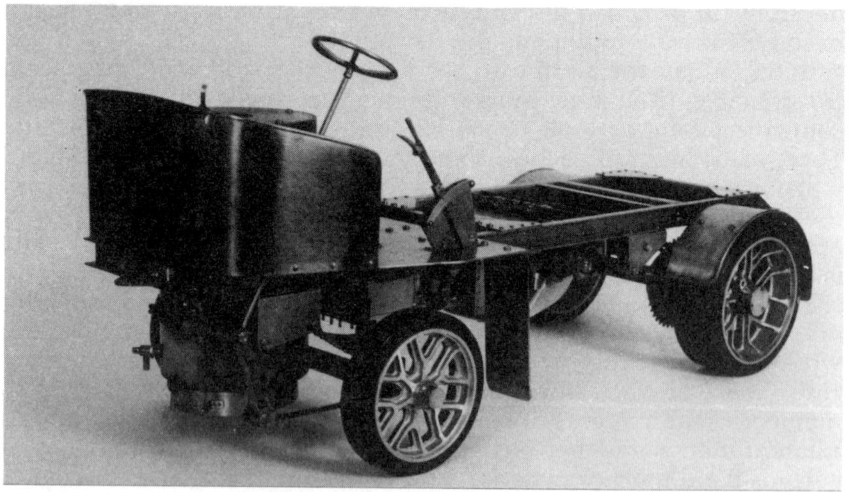

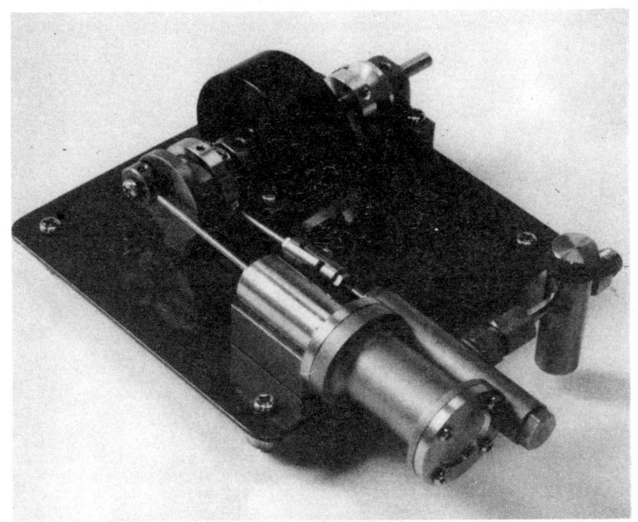

A small and simple piston-valve stationary steam engine, the sort of undertaking that might be considered for a second model.

capacity, capable of drilling accurately. Conversions of D.I.Y. power tools can seldom provide the degree of accuracy needed.

There are scores of accessories available for lathes but the sensible approach is normally to buy an accessory when it is required and if it cannot be made reasonably easily. Most lathe owners would initially set out to acquire a four-jaw independent chuck, a three-jaw self-centring chuck, a tailstock centre, a faceplate (faceplate clamps are straightforward to make) and a tailstock chuck, plus of course three or four of the most-used lathe tools, drills and a centre drill. Add later a mandrel centre and lathe carrier, a machine vice, an assortment of milling cutters and endmills with, preferably, one or two collet chucks to accept their shanks, and a vertical slide, and there will be very few jobs which cannot be successfully carried out.

Hand tools would include screwdrivers, spanners, pliers, snips, hammers etc. common to most home working activities, although it is better to have a set kept for engineering work rather than share them with more mundane household duties. A hacksaw with assorted blades, a junior hacksaw and assorted files are essentials, as is a good solid vice. Small cold chisels and scrapers, centre punches and similar small tools can be made or bought as the need arises; it is even possible to make taps and dies, though most would buy them.

A separate group of tools comprises those needed for measuring and marking out work. Since most model engineering is making one part to fit another and there are accurately-graduated feed dials on

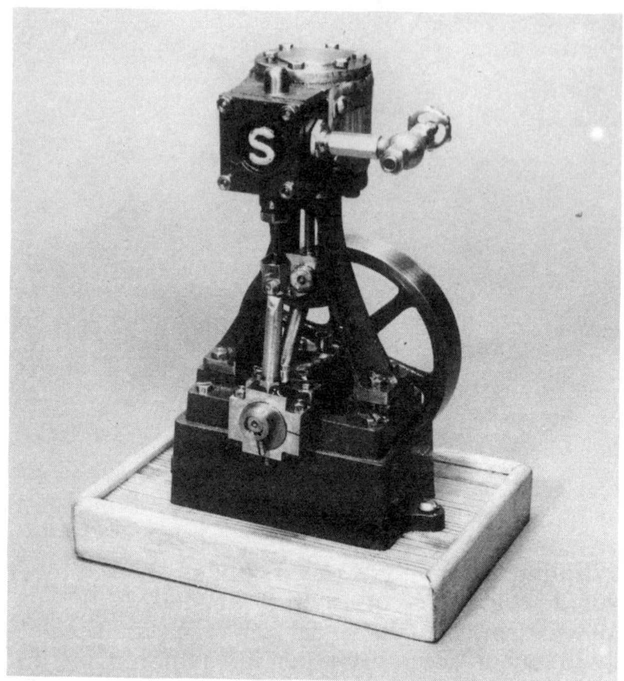

Many thousands of newcomers to model engineering must have built this single-cylinder slide-valve vertical engine as a first project.

the lathe which can be used while work is mounted, only simple tools are essential, though more elaborate ones can be convenient. An engineers' steel rule, outside, inside and odd-leg calipers, a good scriber, dividers, an engineers' square, a fine (60°) dot punch, possibly an adjustable square and a micrometer can, if used correctly, provide just about everything required. Add a pocket calculator, a surface plate (or a sheet of plate glass), a pair of V-blocks, and, for the odd occasion, a vernier gauge (if possible, one of the new ones with digital read-out) and the model engineer is well set up.

What else is needed depends entirely on the direction followed by the individual. If steam is the subject, boilers are involved, which may well mean a brazing hearth, gas/air blowtorch, tongs to handle hot components, a pickle bath and so on. Hearth, tongs and bath can be home-made at no great expense and gas/air equipment can be hired. It may be necessary to have, say, the hind wheels of a traction engine turned elsewhere, because they are too big for the builders' lathe. Castings can be produced at home using a furnace made from an old oil drum, or it may be that facilities for these three examples exist at the local college and can be used at evening classes, or the club workshop may provide them. Model engineering can throw up all sorts of challenges and part of the satisfaction it gives come from finding ways to meet them.

Having discussed the sort of equipment and tools most likely to be needed, it is unfortunate that there is insufficient space in this book to go into how they are used. However, there is an enormous variety of books on all aspects of model engineering work, from basic use of a lathe to specialised books on particular locomotive models or specialised techniques, including many on how to make useful tools, to the extent that given a workshop, materials and a library, a total beginner stranded on a desert island could learn to make a passenger-hauling locomotive or some equally imposing project provided he had common sense and a degree of mechanical aptitude.

Model engineering covers so huge a range of subjects that it defies comprehensive categorisation, but the general areas can be set down and the photographs have been chosen to give perspective to what otherwise might be difficult to visualise.

Stationary steam engines

The origins of model engineering can properly be traced back to atmospheric and early steam engines of the 18th century. There are

A more complex stationary horizontal engine modelled after a full-size machine. Many such engines broken up for scrap with the advent of electric power can now only be seen in model form.

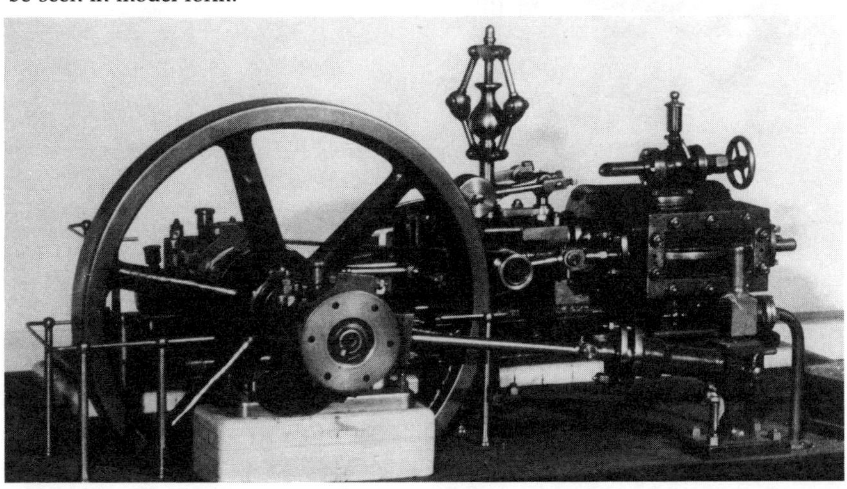

earlier records but rather of novelties than actual models of existing or proposed engines. In a number of cases it is quite clear that a model was built before the full-size engine and that some of the techniques evolved to construct the model were carried over to the large engine and, indeed, to other engineering work.

Examples of contemporary models of mill engines and other machines survive, both in museums and in private collections, and such models have been built in increasing numbers as the years pass. Most are of relatively small and therefore usually simple engines – vertical, horizontal, table, beam etc. – which often form an ideal introduction to the hobby, but outstanding models of large and complex engines are still undertaken by skilled engineers. Many of these enthusiasts served apprenticeships with engine manufacturers and erectors and spent at least the early years of their working lives servicing and maintaining giant steam engines which have only comparatively recently ceased to provide power in textile mills, pumping stations and the like; their models and the descriptive articles written by them in *Model Engineer* make a significant contribution to industrial archaeology.

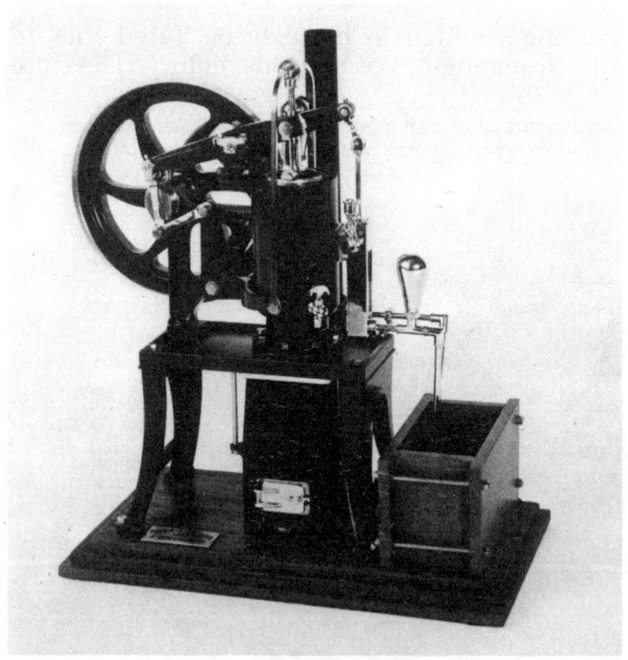

Hot air engines are being researched by several major companies with a view to reintroducing them. This Rider-Ericsson model is typical of a number developed in the 19th century.

Hot air engines

Laymen are often surprised that an engine can run on hot air but such engines have been known for a century or more and were frequently used for pumping duties, in particular. Interest has revived in them in recent years since the heat required can be generated by easily renewable fuels or waste products. Among the research and experiments can be found model engineers whose aim in this instance is not to reproduce machines of the past but to contribute to those of the future.

Marine steam engines

Much of what was said about stationary engines applies here, but in addition to scale models of past engines and their associated plant there is a widespread and growing use of steam propulsion in model boats and, indeed, in passenger-carrying river launches. The first self-propelled models were almost certainly steamboats and steam remained the most popular source of power for larger models until the 1940s, when improved electric and internal combustion motors displaced it. There was little new activity for some 25 years, but then interest reawoke and there are now more commercial steam units available and more people building engines than ever.

Reasons for this new interest include the low cost of operation compared to the average i.c. engine and, provided fuel and water are kept topped up, the virtually limitless operating time. Electric motors share the quiet running advantage but duration of operation is finite, controlled by the need to recharge batteries. There is, too, the special attraction of a steam unit and the inexplicable fascination it exerts over man.

Most boat engines are single cylinder, though examples of two, three or four cylinders are plentiful. The preponderance of the single cylinder arises from the smaller and simpler oscillating engines which are cheaper to make commercially and are perhaps the easiest and quickest form of engine for a beginner to make: it is possible to make one with hand tools only, though the use of a lathe is desirable. More power and greater efficiency is achieved by a slide valve engine, which is not particularly difficult to make but because of higher steam consumption is likely to require slightly more sophisticated boiler and burner arrangements than the simple pot boiler and meths. burner suitable for simple oscillators.

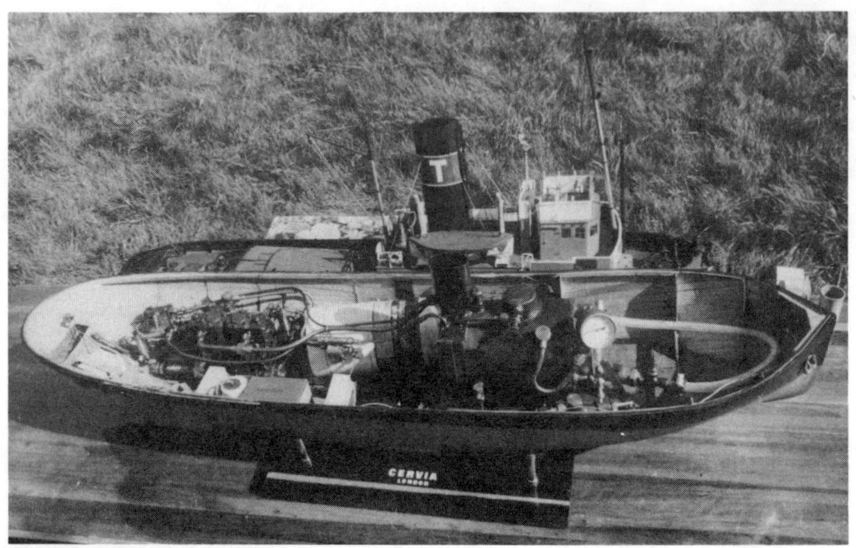

A steam plant in a model tug. Except for the use of silicon rubber sealing rings in place of graphited yarn and gas firing instead of petrol or paraffin, engine and boiler design remain traditional.

Compound and triple-expansion engines are used for model propulsion by some experienced model engineers and there have been many fine models of full-size ships' machinery built as models in their own right rather than for actual use afloat.

Traction engines

Steam power revolutionised farming practice and the general term "traction engines" is widely if incorrectly used to embrace portable engines and ploughing engines and almost any other form of steam engine on three or four wheels capable of moving, or being moved, along roads or over fields. A traction engine proper is a steam tractor used for hauling trailers etc., but most such vehicles were adaptable for other functions such as driving threshing machines or, with crane and dynamo ancillaries, erecting and lighting fairground equipment etc. Steam rollers come under the general heading but steam fire engines do not; the line appears to be drawn between vehicles with wide-rimmed wheels and those with more conventional carriage-type wheels.

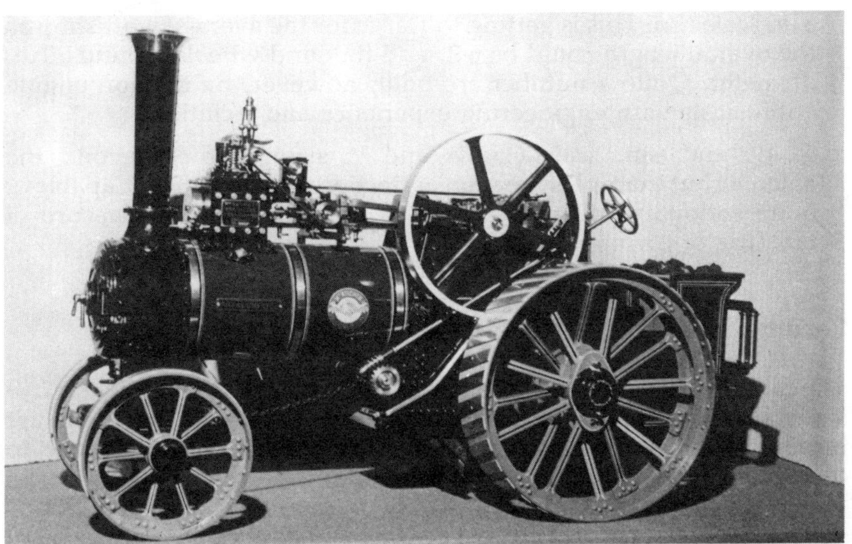

One of the most numerous designs of traction engine models is this 1½in. scale Allchin *Royal Chester*, for which plans, castings and a book of instructions have been available for some twenty years.

The vast majority of traction-engine-type models are self-propelled and enjoy the considerable advantage of not needing a track; they will run on any reasonable surface depending on their size, which can vary from under a foot long (designed to be made on the smaller lathes) to half full size. Most models fit into one or other of the following scales:

1 in. scale (1/12). A very popular size for a beginners' engine, since all components are easily machined on the average lathe and the finished engine is easy to handle and small enough to have on display indoors.

1½ in. scale (⅛). Large enough for the inclusion of all accurate details but still machineable on the average lathe. Should have sufficent power to tow the owner on a driving trolley on asphalt etc.

2 in. scale (1/6). The most popular size for more experienced builders and those who like to see their model performing work. Can be 2½-4 ft. long and weigh well over 1 cwt. (50Kg) and will haul a trailerload of passengers. Hind wheels likely to need a gap-bed 5 in. lathe but remainder can be worked on a 3½ in. machine.

3 in. scale (¼). This is getting too large for the average workshop as the overall length could be 6 ft. and the hind wheels around 20 in. diameter. Quite a number are built, however, by traction engine enthusiasts with engineering experience and facilities.

4, 4½ and 6 in. scale (⅓, ⅜ and ½ size). Rather beyond the amateur but examples are seen at traction engine rallies. Capable of quite serious work, though this is incidental to the pleasure of building or owning one.

Locomotives

The most popular area of model engineering is undoubtedly the live steam locomotive in 3½ or 5 in. gauge, of which at any time there are hundreds under construction. Some, by retired engineers able to devote much of their time to the workshop, are built in as little as 4-6 months, but others take years of patient effort.

Models of locomotives go back to the beginning of the railways, but early models were likely to be the work of apprentices or skilled employees of the builders of the full-size engines. Although amateur-built models from the later part of the 19th century still exist, the growth of the practice as a popular hobby had to wait until the 1920s, when machine tools had become more generally available and a mechanically-minded generation had begun to mature.

Valve gear mechanism, coupling and connecting rods make a complex area on a steam locomotive. As the working of the gear begins to be understood it all becomes simple and logical – and fascinating!

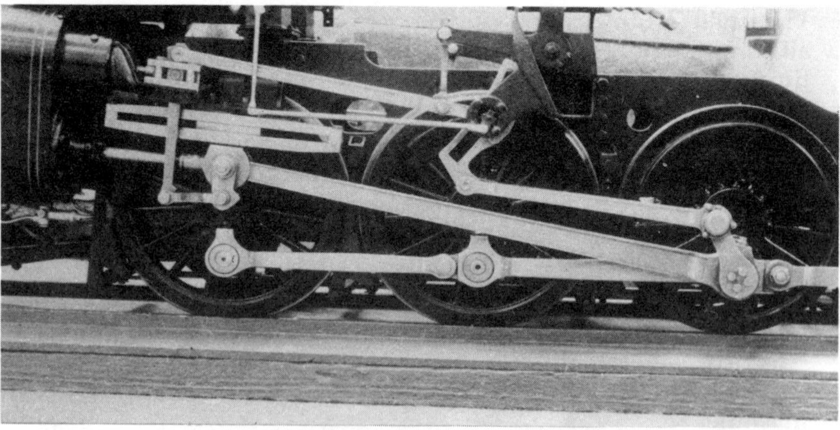

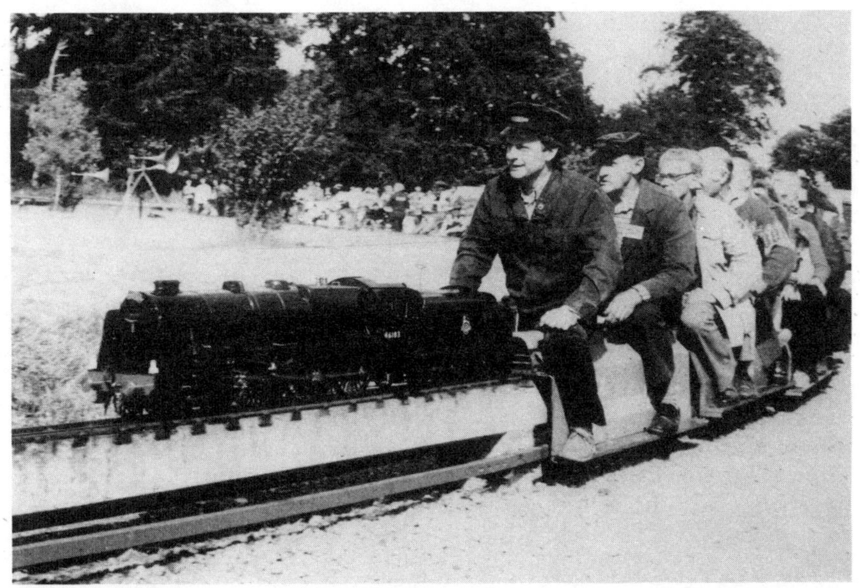

The power of a 5in. gauge locomotive never ceases to surprise people unfamiliar with steam's potential. A good engine will haul up to fifteen adults wih ease on a reasonably level track.

Toy steam locomotives, mostly of German origin, were available around the middle of the 19th century, but these simply ran along the floor. Clockwork mechanisms proved cleaner and safer but track did not appear until the 1890s, again from Germany, and manufacturers in that country produced most of the tinplate British-outline loco- motives sold in Britain up to the First World War. Track standards were variable though a common scale was around 7mm. to 1 ft. (0 gauge) and after about 1915 1¼ in. gradually became standardised as the measure between rails.

Although steam power is possible in 0 gauge, it was a little small for the then state of the art; the early trackless models were larger, about 1¾ in. wheel spacing, and this track gauge enabled steam models to be built and run on garden layouts as Gauge 1. By increasing rail spacing to 2½ in. enough power could be developed by a locomotive to pull its owner along on a trolley, adding a new dimension, and 2½ in. gauge became for many years the size in which model engineers worked. It still retains a following and new designs occasionally appear; drawings for the construction of steam models in 0, 1 and 2½ in. gauge are all easily available.

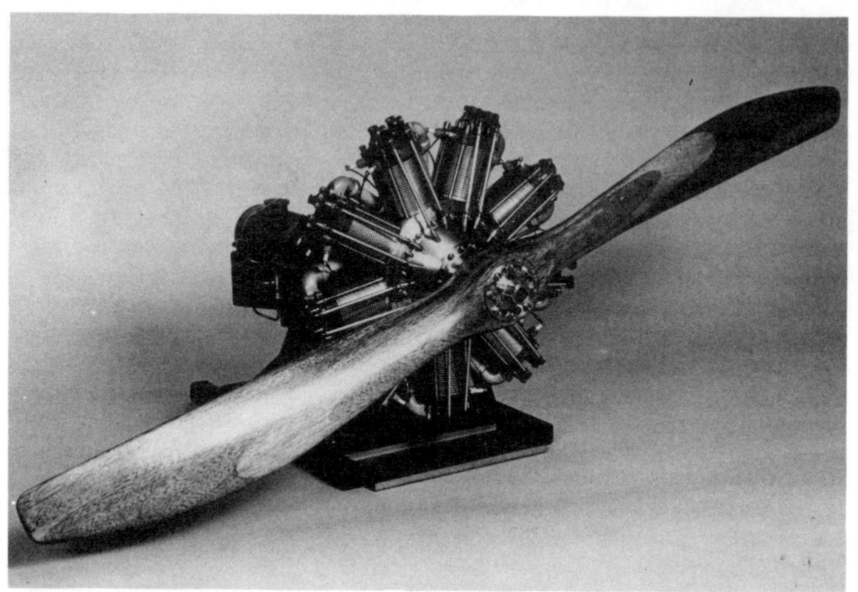

A magnificent example of a working scale engineering model is this Bentley rotary engine. Originally built by an Australian enthusiast, many examples have now been constructed world-wide.

The step to 3½ in. gauge was a logical one, since many of the larger 2½ in. engines exceed in size and weight smaller 3½ in. locomotives, yet the latter are less complex to construct and have adequate power to pull one or two passengers as well as the driver. Before long large prototypes were modelled, with greater passenger-hauling capacity and the step upward was repeated when 5 in. gauge locomotives became accepted as the norm for club track running in the 1950s and 60s. Currently there is a similar situation incipient with 7¼ in. gauge, the next size up, but the average locomotive at this scale is beyond the capacity of the average model engineers' workshop and it therefore does not seem likely that the move will develop fully.

Once the ability to construct a locomotive and actually drive it was realised, individual tracks (often straight lengths) began to seem unsatisfying and few people had sufficient space or time to construct an extensive track. The answer was cooperative effort by club members, on ground provided by local authorities or, if necessary, rented. Part of the cost of materials for construction and/or part of the rental could be recouped by providing rides for the public, which also gave a purpose and discipline to running. Many clubs extended the idea by building a portable track on which fare-paying passengers could ride at charity fetes and similar functions.

Initially some club tracks were for 3½ in. gauge only, and one or two for 5 in. gauge only. However, by using three rails it was found possible to cater for both gauges on the same track-bed and sleepers, and this is more or less standard practice today. It is also normal to have a raised track, about 2 ft. from the ground, for more comfortable driving and attention to the locomotive and wagons. Some tracks are extensive and elaborate, with tunnels, cuttings and viaducts, while others may be simple ovals; most employ coloured light signalling for safety. Carrying members of the public puts a premium on safety and responsible operation, two firm aspects of which are adequate insurance and strict boiler testing and certification.

Once again the benefits of club membership for a beginner are obvious, and he will almost certainly be advised to tackle a simple 0-4-0 or 0-6-0 tank engine for a first locomotive. Such an engine takes less time to build and progress is encouragingly visible. During construction much can be learned by helping at the track and it is usually not long before a keen member is offered the opportunity of learning to drive, either on a club locomotive or on that of a fellow-member.

There is another side to locomotive construction. Some builders derive their pleasure from the actual construction of a working engine as close to scale as possible. On completion the engine is tested and possibly given a run on a track. It is then stripped, painted, reassembled and fitted in a glass case, for loan or sale to a museum or a collector.

Petrol engines

Although this area of model engineering is dominated by petrol (gasoline) engines, it includes most forms of internal combustion engines and the range extends from functional racing glowplug two-strokes to working scale models of full-size aircraft engines. Among outstanding recent examples of the latter are fully operational models of a WW1 Bentley 9 cyl. rotary engine and, even more extraordinary, a 16 cyl. Rolls Royce Merlin.

Many of the drawings and, often, castings available are for four-strokes of one to four cylinders (in-line or opposed pairs) for use in model aircraft or boats, with capacities from the very small (.3cc) to the large, for models (30-50cc).

Clocks

Horology and the making of clocks have in the last few years become sufficiently popular to sustain magazines devoted solely to the subject, but it is still considered a legitimate branch of model engineering, possibly because the size of components and most of the tools required are so similar. Most model engineers have an interest in clocks but only a relatively small number actually engage in their construction.

Tools

It has been said that some model engineers spend so much time making tools to make models that they never get around to the actual model! This is of course an exaggeration, but there is no denying that some practitioners find the development of special tools an irresistible challenge. Some of these tools and attachments are adopted by

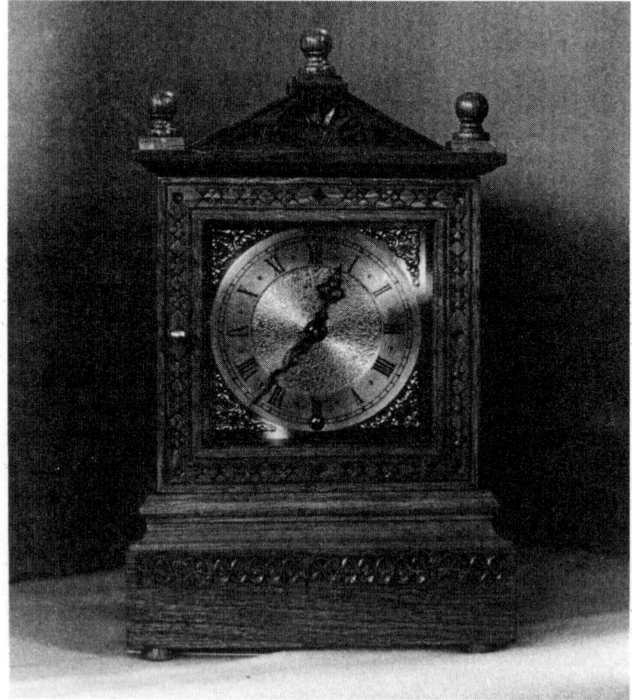

Clock-making may seem a strange part of model engineering but there are close associations. This handsome oak mantle clock was made by J. A. Jowitt.

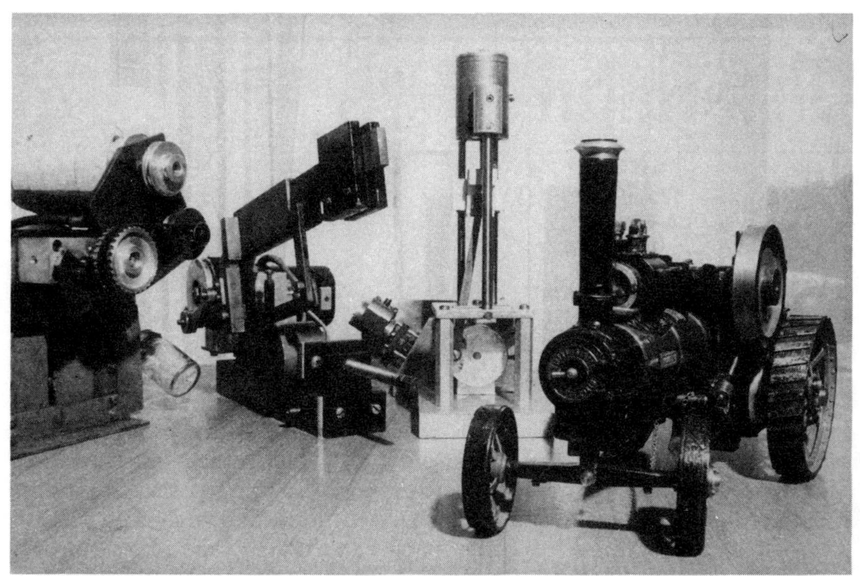

A small workshop compressor, a power hacksaw, an experimental steam engine
and a tiny steam-powered traction engine, all produced on a miniature 1¾in. lathe by
Rex Tingey, show what can be done.

industry but often the only reward the originator receives – or seeks –
is the satisfaction of knowing that he has solved a problem.

"Tools" is a somewhat loose term which embraces anything from a
simple scribing block to a lathe toolholder or precision boring head
right up to complete machines such as Professor Chaddock's "Quorn"
tool and cutter grinder. Some merely save the necessity to purchase:
miniature cold chisels, for example, can be ground from pieces of
broken mechanical hacksaw blade. Others do a job which would
otherwise mean a special and expensive purchase, and an example
here is the simple task of making a D-bit from steel rod which will
finish a hole accurately enough to avoid the need to buy a reamer
which might neve be used again. It is not difficult to make a pillar drill
or a bench grinder or a power hacksaw providing you have the basic
lathe and the time.

Electrical devices, instruments, tramcars, horse-drawn vehicles,
artillery and many other facets classed under "model engineering"
have not been described, the difficulty being to know where to stop!
Perhaps, however, some glimpse has been given of the varied and
fascinating world which is open to anyone with a mechanical turn of
mind.

Ulsterman

Appendix 1

This little model is an exercise in simple balsa construction, not very costly to make but capable of providing hours of amusement on the pond. It can be run free but is just big enough to accept small modern radio-control equipment to provide steering; motor speed control would be possible for an experienced modeller but is not recommended for a beginner because space is a little limited.

The general appearance is based on an offshore oil rig tender but it makes no pretence to be a scale model. It is deliberately made wider and deeper to accept radio or ballast weight to provide stable performance with a very simple hull form. One advantage of it being non-scale is that the builder can leave off or add details as he pleases and can use any colour scheme he prefers.

Basic requirements are two sheets of ⅛x3x36 in. medium-to-soft balsa, a balsa knife, pins and a tube of balsa cement. A small amount

Ulsterman on trials. The prototype's hull and motor weighed only 3½ ounces (ca. 100 gms) and with batteries and ballast totalling a further 20 ozs had quite a lively performance.

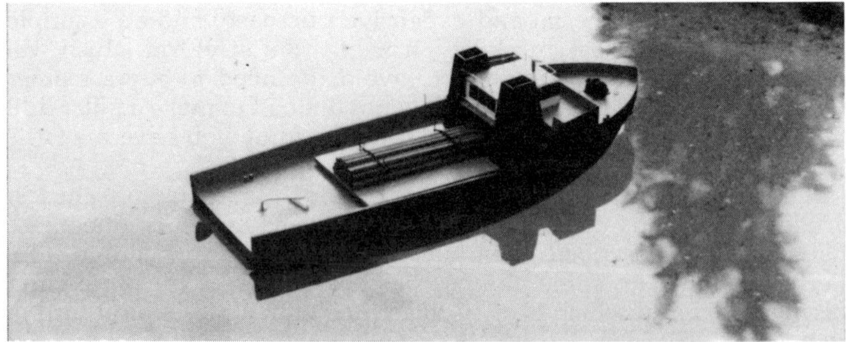

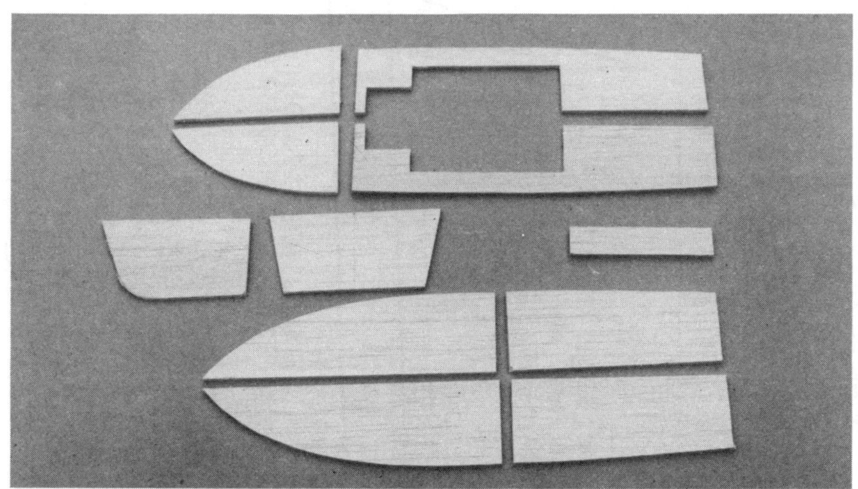

The eleven basic hull pieces, seven of which have to be traced from the full-size parts shown on pages 118-119. A photocopy of each of the drawings will save spoiling the book.

of ⅟₁₆ in. balsa is also needed and you may be able to buy a damaged sheet or one of the "balsa packs" made up as a bundle of short lengths in a variety of sizes. Later stages will require sanding sealer, tissue and clear dope if you wish, and small quantities of paint. A small propeller shaft and tube and a small electric motor completes the list, as other odds and ends will be found around the house. If the items are purchased over two or three weeks the cost will hardly be noticed; completing the hull up to installing the shaft tube cost £1.08 on the original model, including cement, but you could spend £2 on sealer and paint.

The hull frame consists of 11 pieces of ⅛ in. balsa, four of which are opposite-hand pieces, so there are only 7 to mark out. These are shown full-size and can be traced with a soft pencil on to kitchen greaseproof paper which is then turned over, positioned on the wood and the lines drawn over on the back, transferring the original lines. Or you can use carbon paper under the plan to draw paper or card templates, or if you have access to a dry photo-copier, simply make a copy of the drawing. The shapes can either be cut out of the copy or the copy placed face-down on the wood and a warm iron rubbed across the paper, which will transfer the lines.

Cut out with a sharp blade, using three or four strokes rather than trying to cut through in one. Use a steel rule or the smooth edge of a hacksaw blade to guide the knife on straight lines, but cut the curves

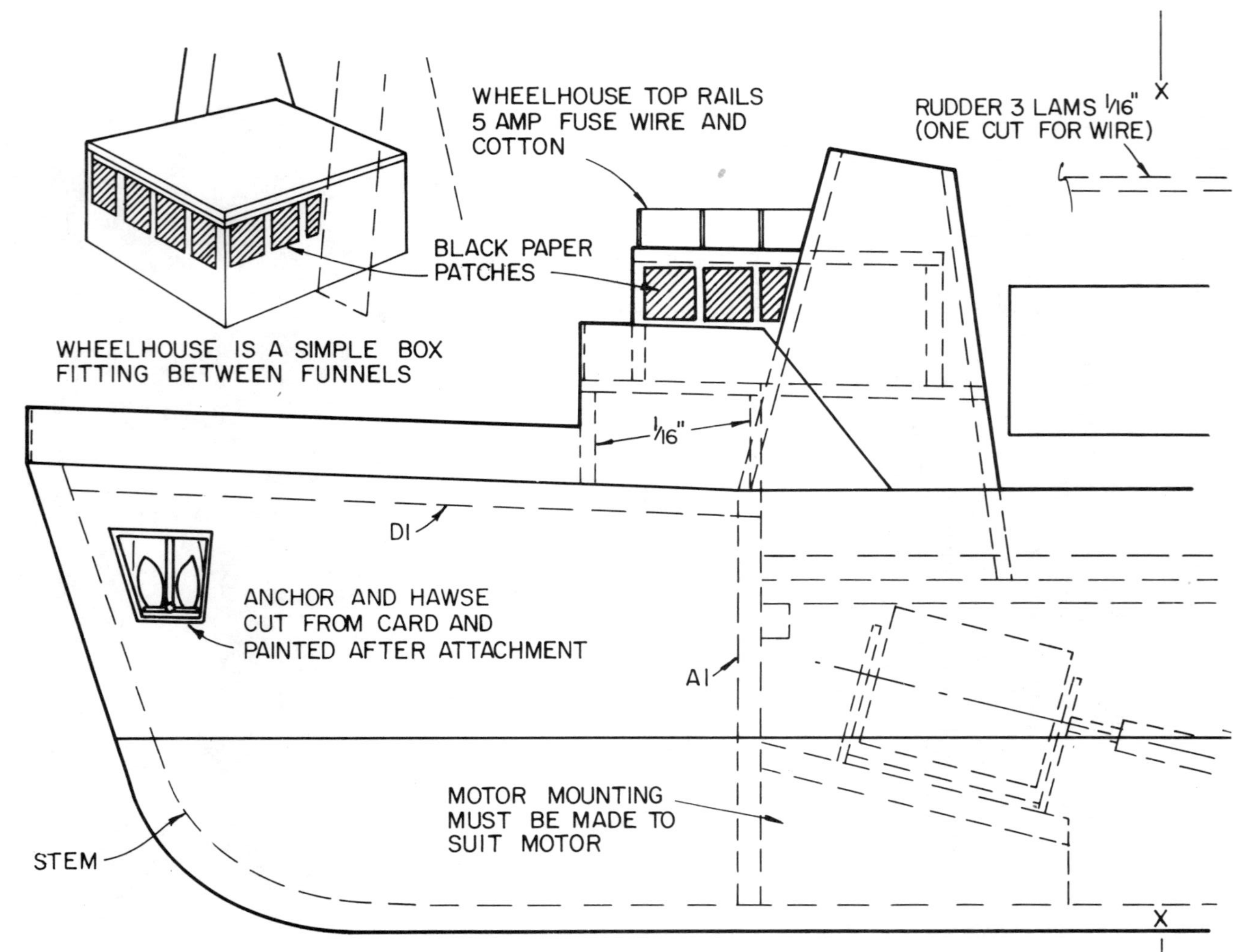

WHEELHOUSE TOP RAILS
5 AMP FUSE WIRE AND
COTTON
RUDDER 3 LAMS 1/16"
(ONE CUT FOR WIRE)
BLACK PAPER
PATCHES
WHEELHOUSE IS A SIMPLE BOX
FITTING BETWEEN FUNNELS
1/16"
DI
ANCHOR AND HAWSE
CUT FROM CARD AND
PAINTED AFTER ATTACHMENT
AI
STEM
MOTOR MOUNTING
MUST BE MADE TO
SUIT MOTOR
X
X
110

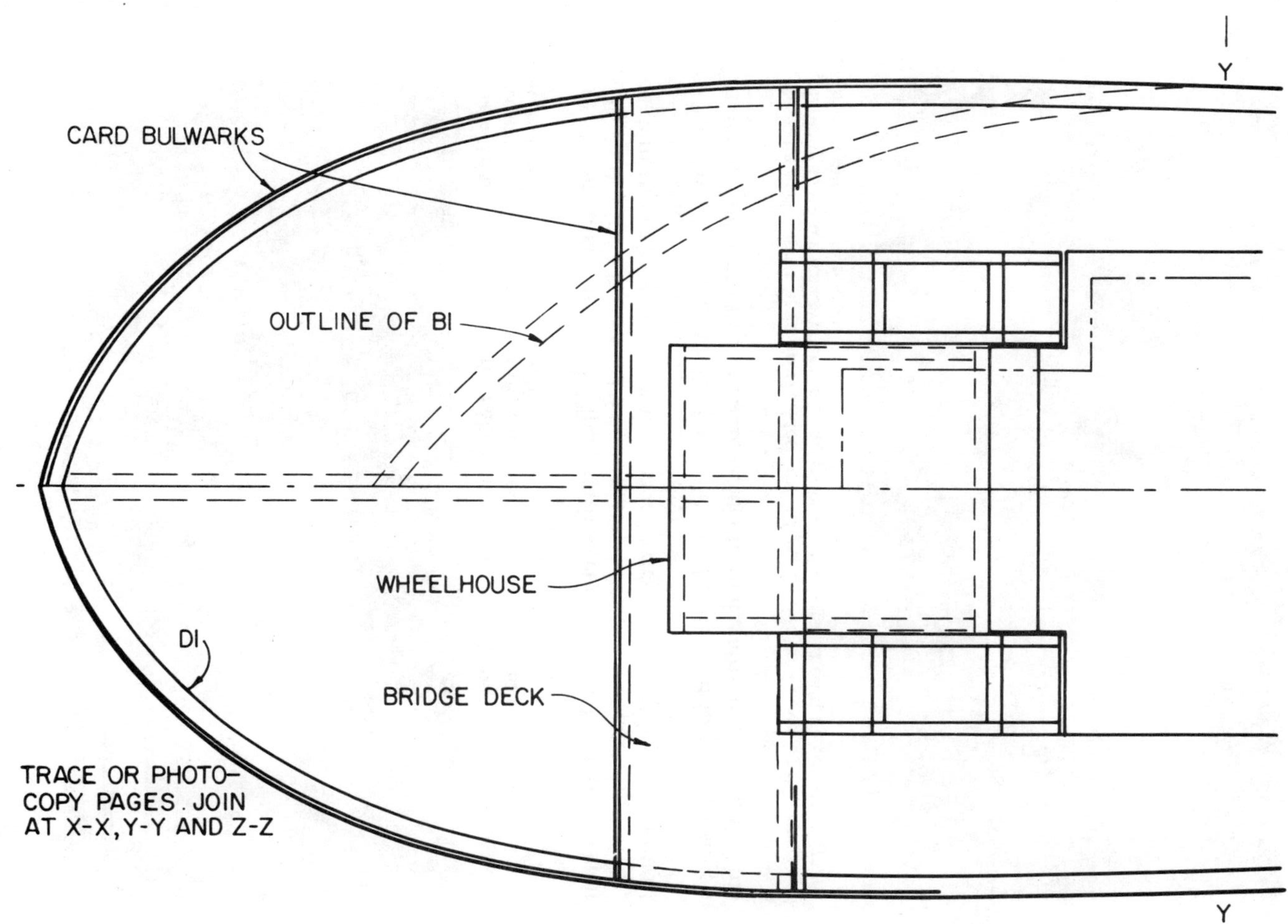

CARD BULWARKS
OUTLINE OF BI
WHEELHOUSE
BRIDGE DECK
DI
TRACE OR PHOTO-
COPY PAGES. JOIN
AT X-X, Y-Y AND Z-Z
Y
Y

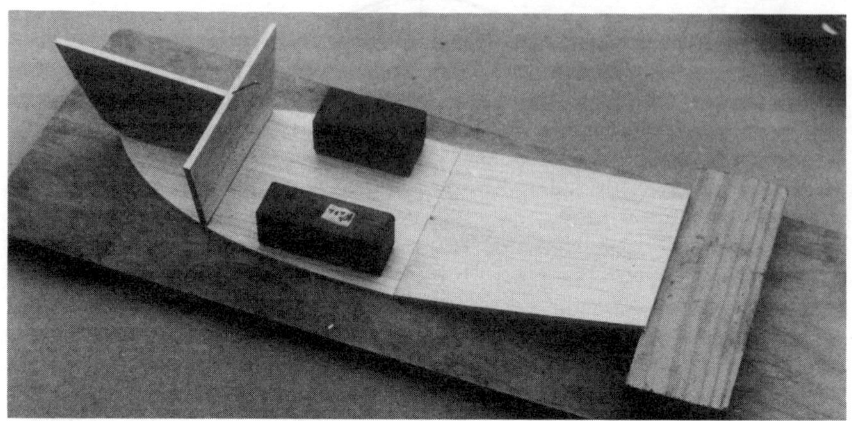

Use a flat board to assemble the hull frame and be sure that the stern end is raised accurately to the height given. A school set-square can be used to check that everything is assembled squarely.

free-hand, just outside the line, with several light cuts. Use the half panels B1, B2, D1 and D2 as templates to cut their matching halves, cement the halves together and leave to dry. After cutting A1, cement a scrap strip of balsa across as shown.

Now mark where A1 fits across B1 and cement it in place, using a matchbox or some small square object to make sure it is upright. This

Here the deck pieces have been added, the edges sanded to a bevel as described and planking is under way. Where the curves begin the balsa should be cut into narrow strips, grain top to bottom.

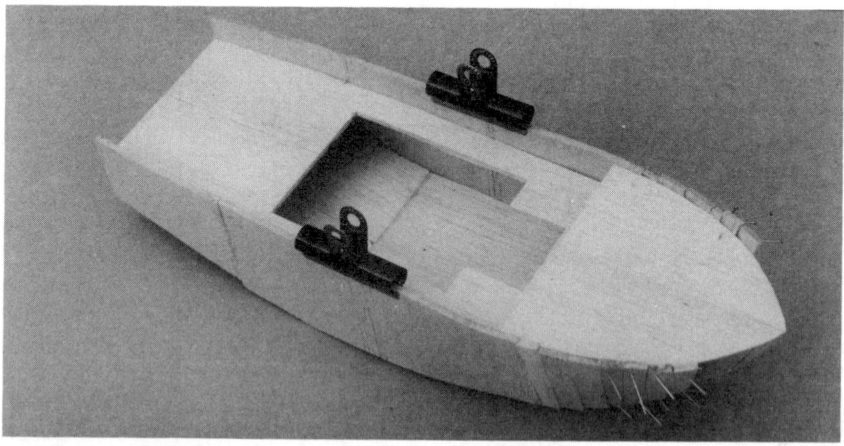

and subsequent steps should be carried out with B1 laid flat – even lightly pinned with dressmakers' pins – to a small flat board which can be covered with waxed paper or clingfilm so that cement does not stick to it. Cement the stem in place, straight and central, pinning temporarily with a pin through the top of A1. Lightly sand a bevel in the joint end of B2 and cement to B1, blocking up the stern end $\frac{7}{8}$ in. (22m) with a strip of wood as shown in the photograph.

When dry cement on D1, the after edge of which is flush with A1. Also position A2 and cement D2 in place, resting on the piece of scrap on the aft face of A1 and the top of A2. Pins can be used to hold parts while the cement dries, then withdrawn. Leave the structure for several hours, preferably overnight.

Wrap a piece of fairly fine glasspaper round a piece of wood about 6 n. long. Lift the model frame off the board and lightly sand the deck and bottom edges all the way along each side, using the sanding block to sand deck and bottom edges simultaneously. Towards the bow this will introduce an increasing bevel along the edges.

Now cut a piece off the $\frac{1}{8}$ in. sheet remaining, $2\frac{1}{8}$ in. or a fraction more long, giving a $3 \times 2\frac{1}{8}$ in. piece with the grain the short way. Cement this vertically to one side of the hull at the stern with $\frac{1}{2}$ in. or so projecting above deck level and the after edge flush with the outside face of A2. If you prefer, the bottom edge of this piece can be cut to match the angle of the hull bottom. Cut a second piece and cement on the opposite side. A pin at each corner will hold these pieces while the cement dries.

It is easier to work the bow planking with the hull upside-down. Strips are better too long than too short, as they can be trimmed and sanded smooth when planking is completed. Note the stem is bevelled.

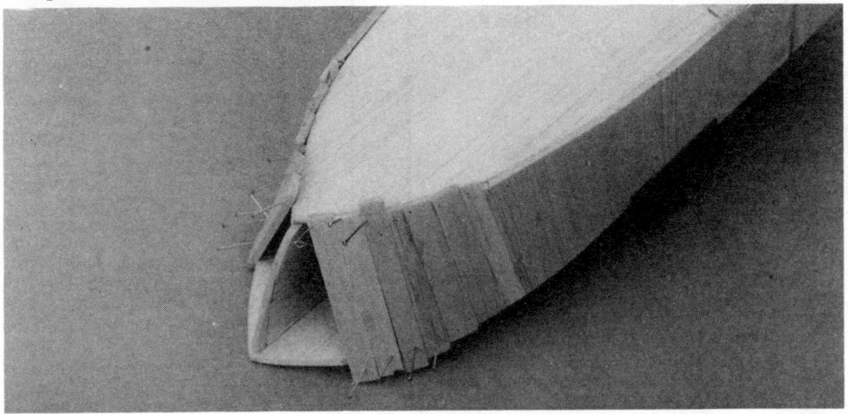

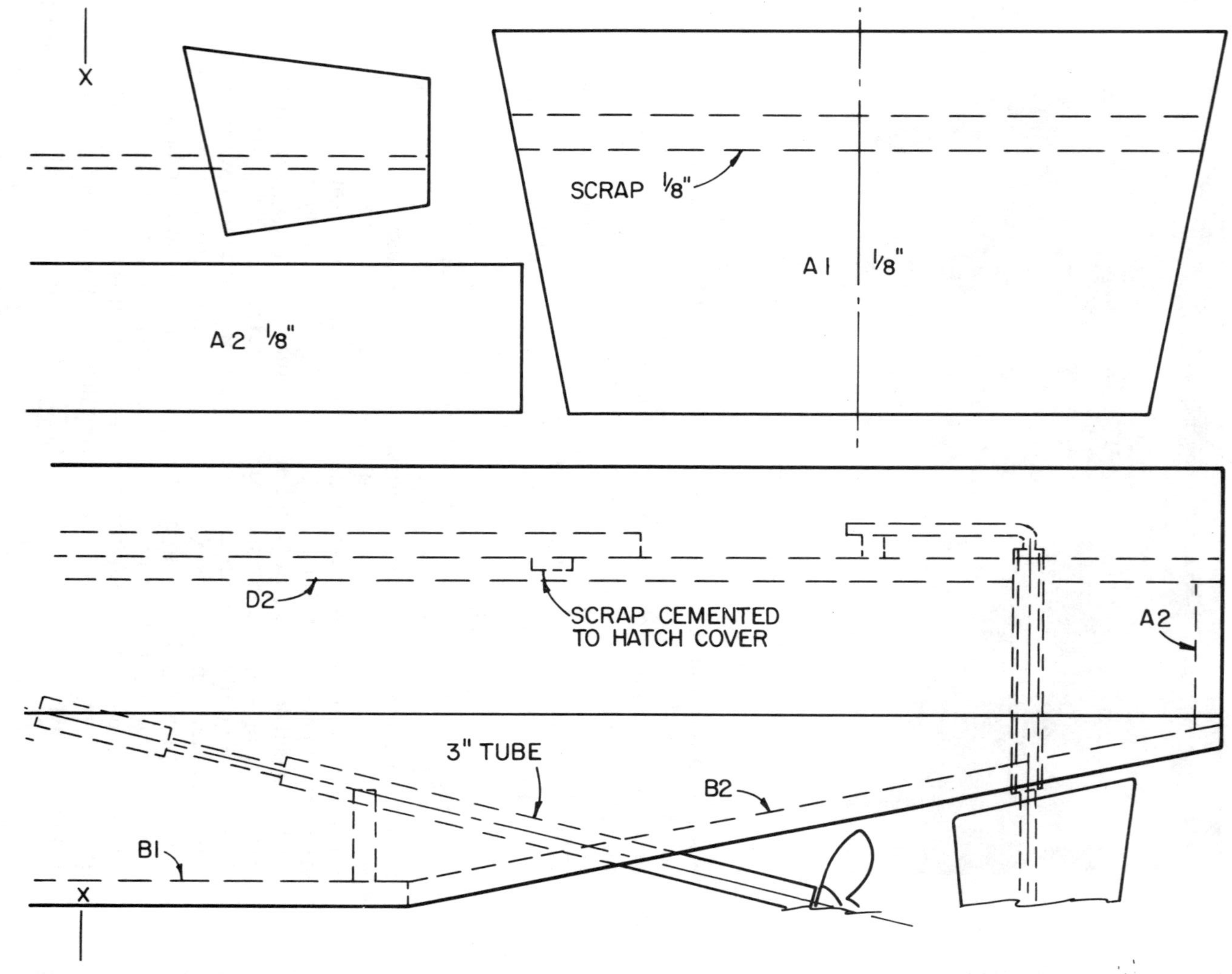
X
SCRAP 1/8"
A1 1/8"
A 2 1/8"
D2
SCRAP CEMENTED
TO HATCH COVER
A2
3" TUBE
B2
B1
X

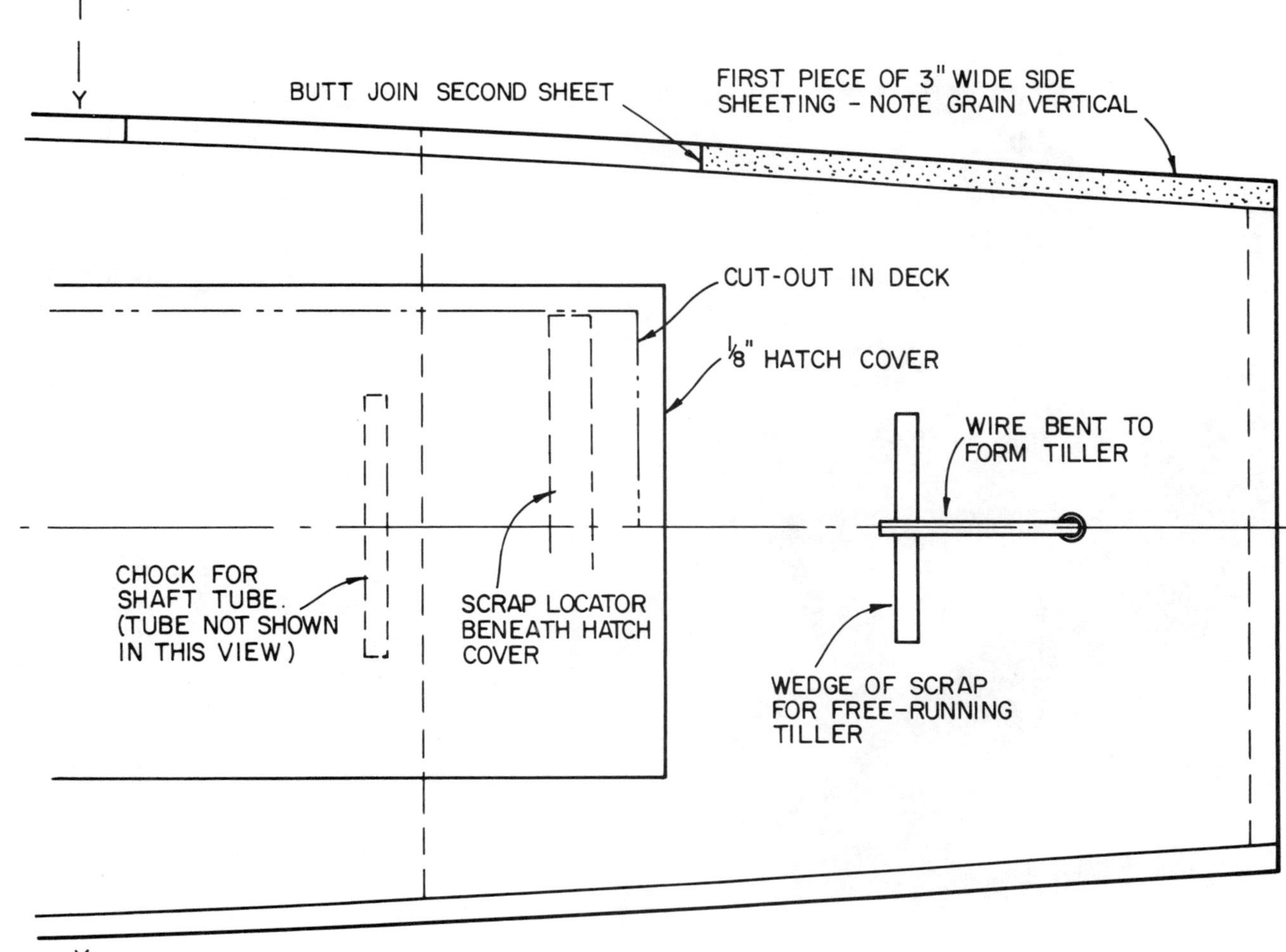

BUTT JOIN SECOND SHEET
FIRST PIECE OF 3" WIDE SIDE SHEETING - NOTE GRAIN VERTICAL
CUT-OUT IN DECK
1/8" HATCH COVER
WIRE BENT TO FORM TILLER
CHOCK FOR SHAFT TUBE. (TUBE NOT SHOWN IN THIS VIEW)
SCRAP LOCATOR BENEATH HATCH COVER
WEDGE OF SCRAP FOR FREE-RUNNING TILLER
Y
Y
115

Cut two more pieces off the 3 in. width for the next sheets to be applied: these will need to be a little deeper, as the hull depth has increased. Again cement one piece each side, projecting above deck and cementing the edges to the previous pieces, then cut two more pieces, which will be 2⅜ in. long as the fore ends have to extend over B1 and D1. You may find that the wood will not twist enough to sit easily, in which case cut ½ in. wide vertical strips off and cement them on separately. Strips of this width can be twisted in the fingers, gently, and held for a few moments (or even breathed on), when they will lie properly in place. From here to the stem use strips all the way, cutting them as narrow as necessary to ensure that they seat reasonably. Overhang at top and bottom will be trimmed off later.

Strips meeting on the stem will need to be bevelled to butt against each other neatly, and it is best to cut long strips, fit the bevel and cement in place, then cut excess strip off. If you bought medium/soft balsa this is quite a pleasant bit of construction which is very

The funnels, bridge structure and wheelhouse are now in position on the sanded hull. The ends of the bridge 'box' are open, but will be covered by the card bulwarks, which can be tackled next.

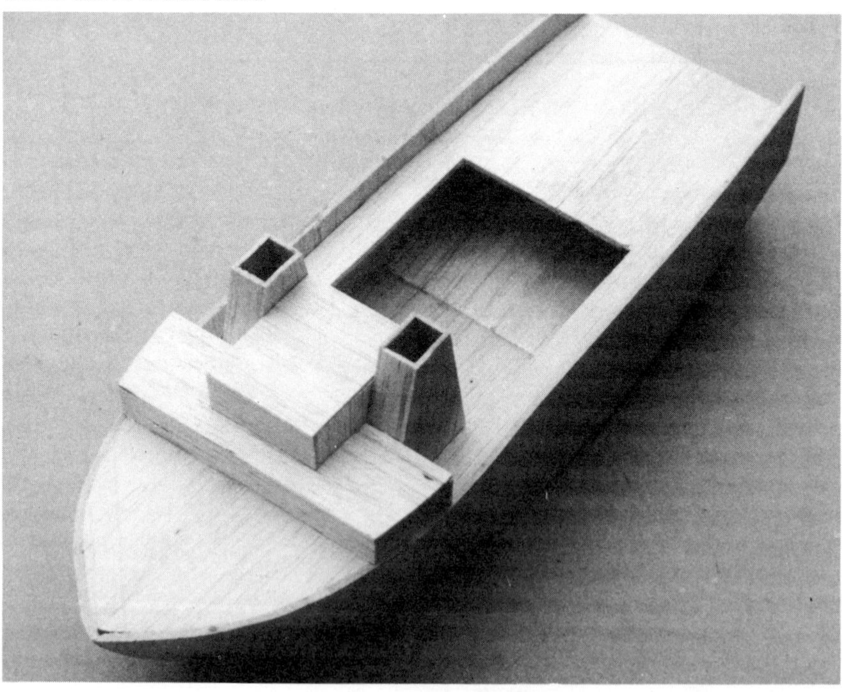

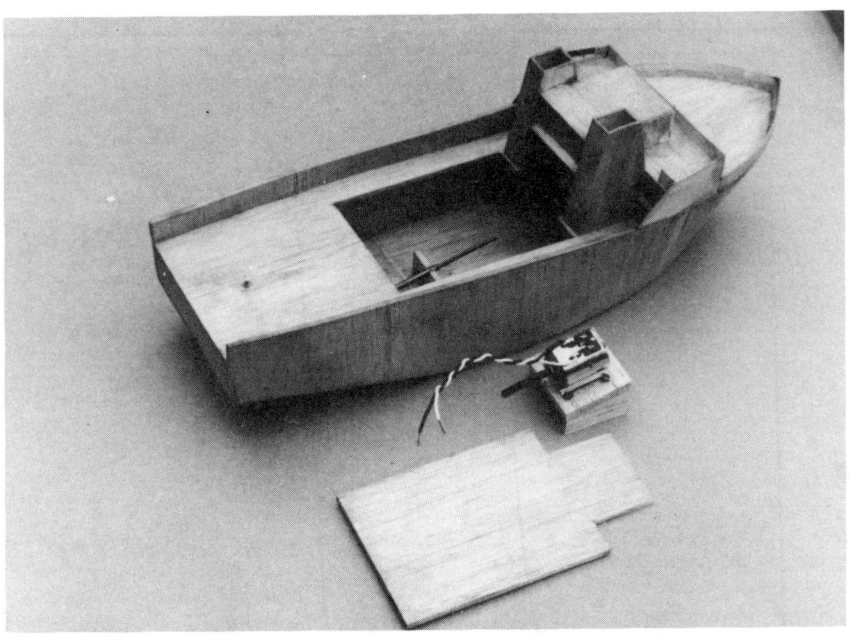

Here the bulwarks have been cut and fitted, the propeller shaft and rudder tube installed, a hatch cover cut and the motor mounted ready to instal once the interior has been painted with sealer.

rewarding when sanded smooth, but if your balsa is hard it becomes more tedious, since the strips will have to be narrower. Trim away excess along the bottom edge and above D1 with a sharp blade and fine glasspaper. Above D2 the side skins form bulwarks about ½ in. high, so clamp a strip of wood ½ in. thick on the inside and trim and sand down to this. The main hull can now be put temporarily aside.

Trace and cut one funnel profile from 1/16 in. balsa and use this to cut three more. Cut some strips ⅜ in. wide and assemble two funnels by cementing the strips between pairs of sides, flush with the edges. Cut two strips a bare ½ in. wide and cement one on edge across D1 to continue the line of A1 upwards, and the second also on edge across D1 at the forward edge of the bridge deck. Trace and cut the bridge deck and cement in place on the two strips. Make the wheelhouse from four sides of 1/16 in. plus the top. You can if you wish paint all these parts with sanding sealer, rub down with very fine glasspaper or, better, carborundum paper, repeat, then paint them before assembly. This helps to get sharp paint lines.

Cement the wheelhouse in place, then check the funnels for fit and

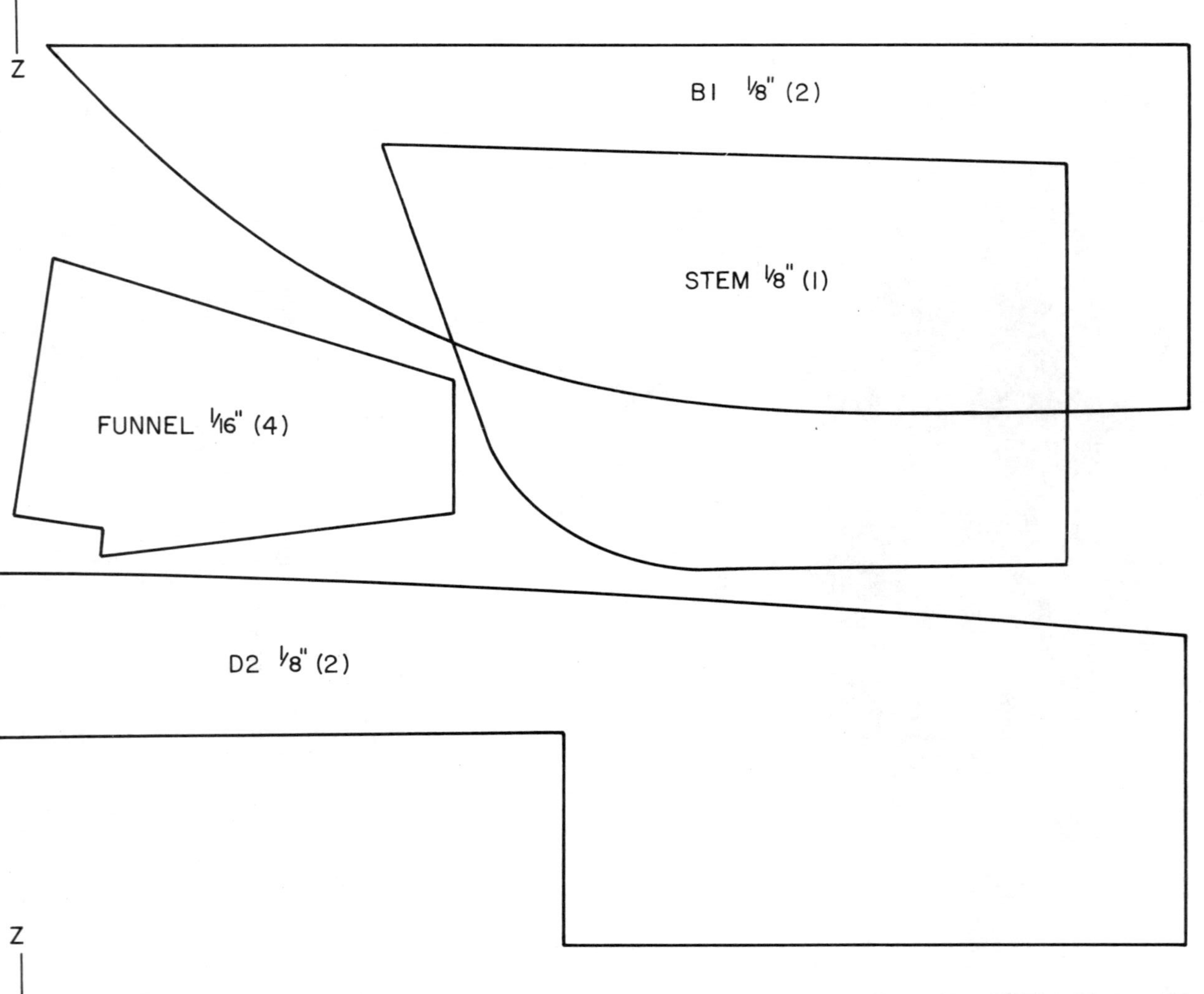

118

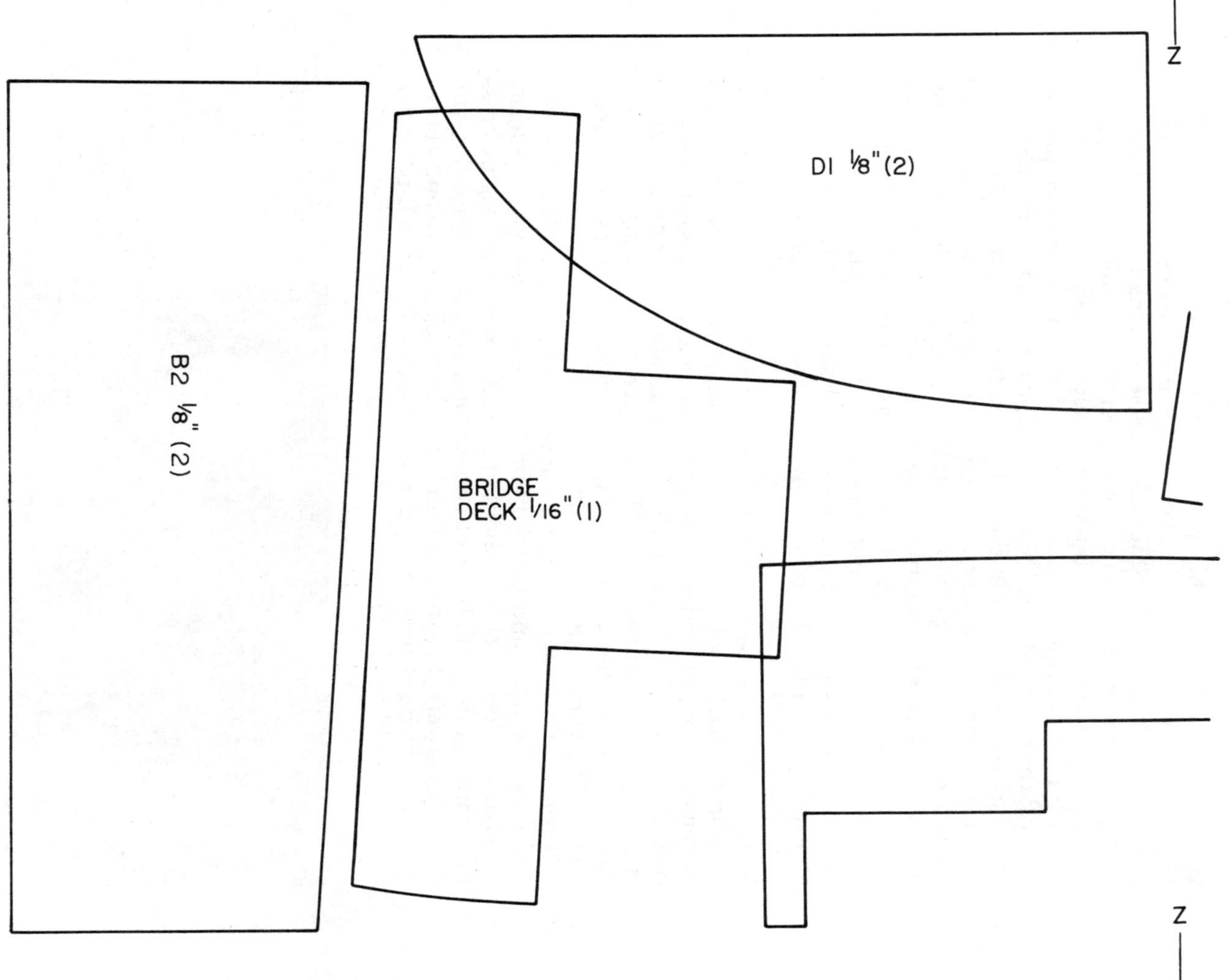

119

cement one each side. The wheelhouse windows may be cut from black paper and stuck on at a later stage, but it would be possible to use card or plastic card for the wheelhouse, cutting the windows out and glazing them with celluloid inside before assembly. If you go this far you may wish to furnish the wheelhouse interior. . .

The bridge deck bulwarks are cut from card – the uncreased parts of a cereal carton will do well. Cut the bridge deck ends and make sure that they will lie flush with the hull sides, trimming the balsa bridge structure as necessary. Cement on, but do not use excessive cement as shrinking on drying could distort the card. Cut and cement a strip across the foreside and two little pieces aft, as illustrated. The foredeck bulwarks are cut to fit and curved in the fingers before cementing on; they are quite firm when dry and painted, but little triangular knees can be fitted inside if desired. All these card bits should be cut with a sharp blade and straightedge, not with scissors.

To complete the basic woodwork a hatch cover is needed, and this is cut from ⅛ in. sheet to a sliding fit between the funnels and should overlap the hatch by ⅛ in. all round. A scrap of ⅛ or 1/16 in. should be cemented on the underside towards the rear to position it centrally over the hatch. Note that such a cover is not watertight, so avoid splashing water on the deck. The absence of a bulwark across the stern, which is often a feature of tenders handling pipes and cables, helps in allowing water to run off.

It is as well to make the rudder at this stage, as the blade is wood and it can be filled and painted with the rest of the model. Ideally brass or stainless steel wire should be used, running through a brass tube through the hull, but for economy it is possible to use the wire from a lightweight coat-hanger or a giant size paper clip and almost any tube which is strong enough; the metal tube from a ball-point pen refill is one obvious source. The wire should be roughened with a file

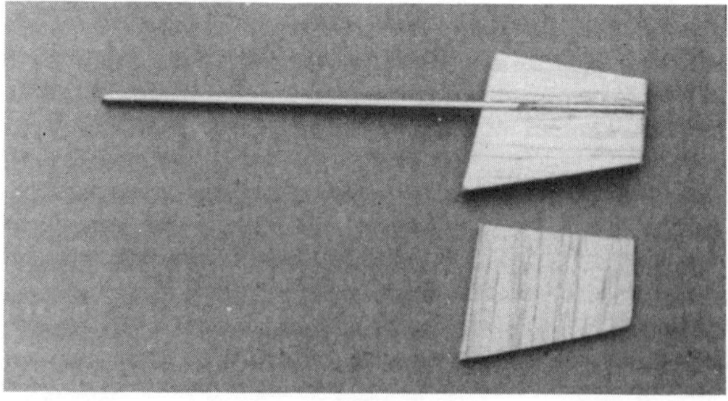

The centre rudder lamination, with the wire glued in place, and one of the side laminations. Note grain is at right-angles.

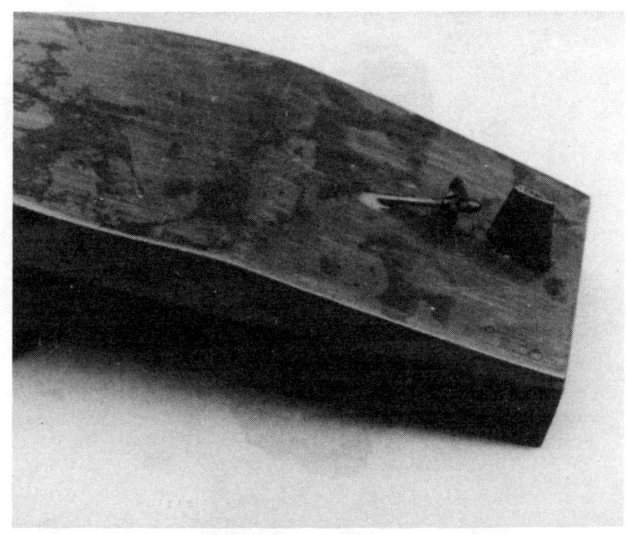

Rudder and propeller on the finished model; blotchy appearance is water, since boat had just completed first trials.

at the bottom end and cemented between two pieces of 1/16 in. sheet as shown, with a further single piece each side and left under a weight to dry. The rudder can then be sanded to shape, sealed and painted etc. A drill, or a wire, should be passed through the hull to make holes top and bottom for the tube, the tube cut to length, its ends roughened and then the length cemented into the hull, using a fillet of cement top and bottom to make it watertight.

A small propeller unit with a 3 in. tube can be bought or another pen refill used for the tube with a piece of bicycle spoke for the shaft and a propeller cut from tinplate soldered on. The best tool to make a suitable hole in B2 is a round needle file but it can be done with a drill twirled in the fingers. Check the angle carefully, then roughen and cement in the tube. Apply cement fillets inside and out when the initial cement is dry. Note the little chock inside which steadies the tube and helps to achieve the correct angle.

An Orbit 005 electric motor running on 1.5 to 3 volts was used on the original, but any small low voltage motor with an armature diameter of ½ in. or a little less can be used. It should be mounted on a ply or balsa plate (two thicknesses of ⅛ in. would be suitable) and secured by screws, if it has feet, or by cementing a screw in each side of the plate and looping a rubber band back and forth between them, over the motor case. The plate is cemented to two tapered cheeks and these should be trimmed or packed so that the motor shaft is exactly in line with the propeller shaft. Spend time getting this right, as it will

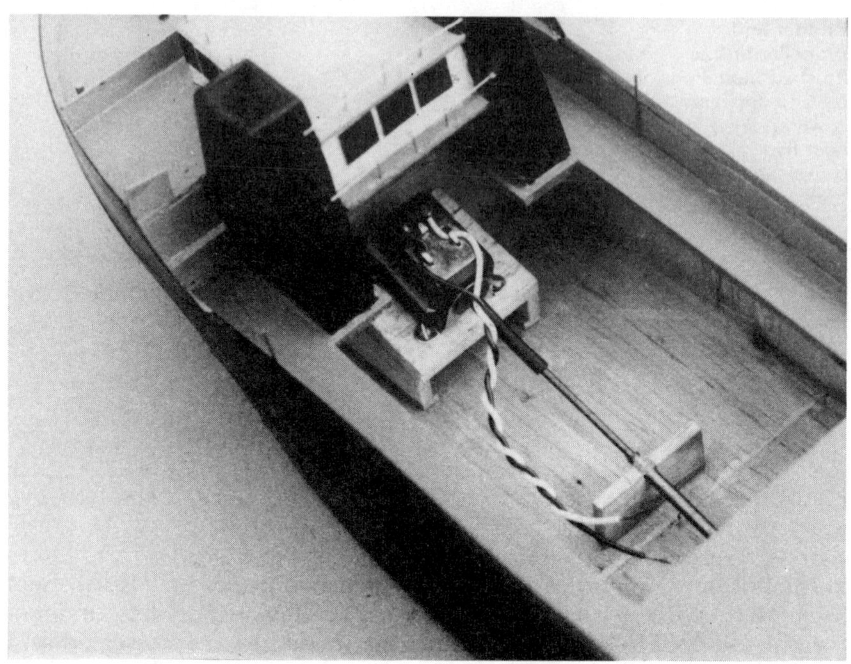

The motor finally installed and awaiting connection to a battery box. There is room and weight allowance for radio control. Black paper windows on wheelhouse and a rail between the funnels can be seen. A ladder to the bridge deck against each funnel has yet to be added.

affect both the boat's speed and the battery life. On a little model like this the shafts can be connected with a piece of flexible plastic tube, one source of which is the insulation sleeving from electrical cable. Check that rotation is free before finally cementing the motor mounting in place.

Now seal the whole model, inside and out, with two coats of sanding sealer and rub down the outside, applying further coats until the grain is all filled. For long life it is worth then tissue-covering the hull exterior, ideally with model aircraft tissue but a fine paper handkerchief would do. Lay the tissue in place and brush clear dope (or sanding sealer) over it, seal a further coat, rub down and it is ready to paint.

Mark the waterline by holding a soft pencil on a block of wood of appropriate thickness and sliding it round the hull while it is held firmly on a flat surface. The line can be masked with cellophane tape, but first run the tape between the finger and thumb to reduce its

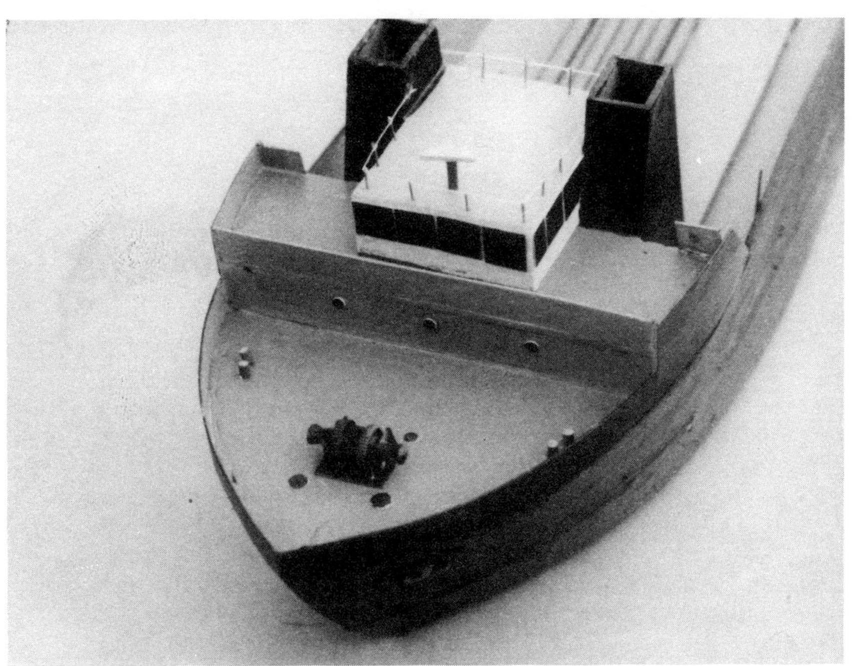

Ports and hawse-holes are punched from black paper with a leather punch,
windlass is from discarded lighter wheels, three scraps of card and two airgun slugs.
Bollards are lengths cut from a pre-painted cocktail stick, anchors from card, rail
from fuse-wire stanchions and cotton.

stickiness slightly. Alternatively use gummed paper and soak it off
after painting. A dark grey or black hull with a red oxide or dark
green bottom looks well. The decks can be dull red, green or grey,
inside of bulwarks red or grey, funnels almost anything, wheelhouse
white or brown – in other words, there is a very wide choice. Colour
photos of full-size tenders (try the library) may provide help. Use
matt paints for best effect, incidentally.

Details are also wide open. An anchor windlass would be sited on
the foredeck and can be made from the wheels from discarded
cigarette lighters plus laundry studs etc. Bollards or bitts and mooring
posts can be dowel. Rails round the wheelhouse top can be short
lengths of thin wire cemented into pinholes with fine copper strands
(from household flex) cemented on. Whip aerials can be broom
bristles (less dangerous than wire) and radar scanners made from
card and dowel. Liferaft containers can also be dowel. A waterfall
winch could be tucked under the bridge deck between the funnels,

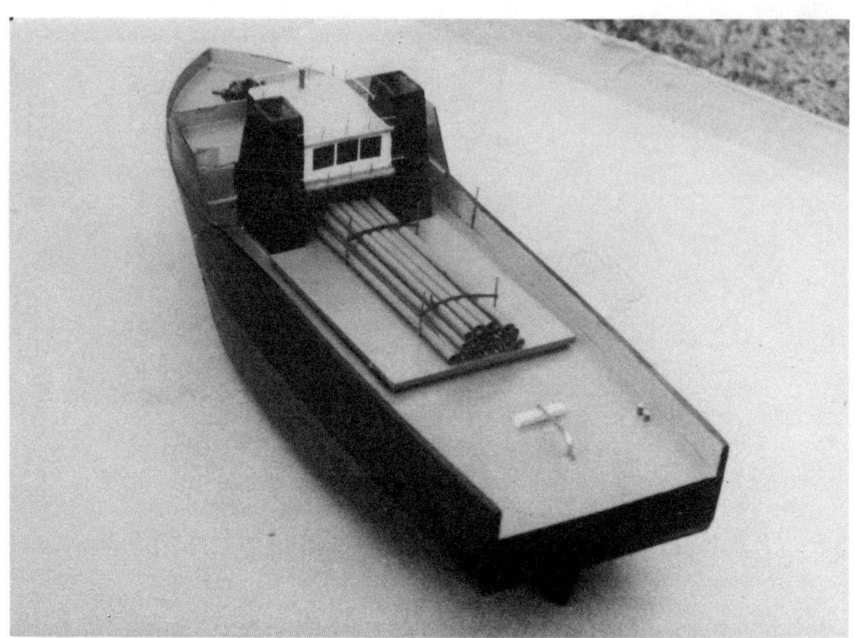

A load of pipes, made from painted drinking straws, would be typical for this type of vessel. Glue, plus painted headless pins and shirring elastic loops, hold them in place. Crates and drums and other details can be added to choice; no doubt builders will have ideas.

using a plastic cotton spool for the main drum. A deck cargo of pipes, made from painted drinking straws, plus drums from dowel would add interest. Stockless anchors could be made from card, cocktail sticks or split matchsticks and cemented in shallow squares cut at the bow, but not right through the planking, using paint to give an illusion of depth. Which then takes us to rust streaks beneath the anchors and general weathering or rusting of the rest of the model. . . the scope is endless.

For a model which will be run frequently it is worth painting the whole of it with a coat of thin matt or satin polyurethane varnish, which will not show but which will make the model's surfaces tougher and easier to keep clean.

If radio control is installed, mount the rudder servo under the deck aft of the hatch with the disc or arm poking through the deck and a short push-rod to the tiller. This could all be concealed under a wooden crate, which itself would be fun to model. The receiver and battery should be tucked away towards the stern and a short aerial

124

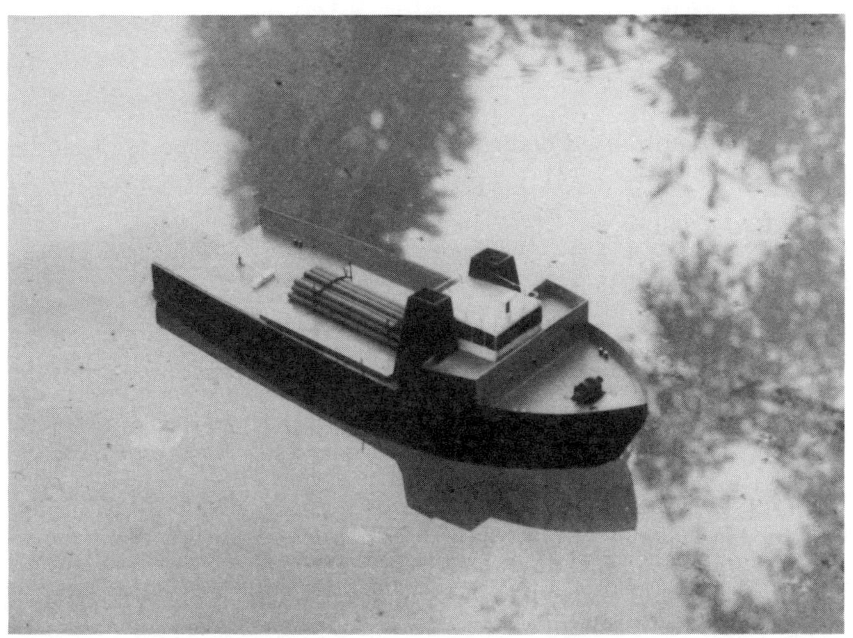

Floating on its waterline and ready to respond to the switch-on. Action shots of the model were scheduled to appear in the first programme of the six-part Ulster TV series, 'Model Magic'. No doubt existing model boat enthusiasts will build one for fun competitions.

laid along the deck; although shortening the aerial reduces range the model is unlikely to be operated at a great distance.

Main motor batteries might be two U2 dry cells or equivalent, or two 1·2v 1·2a/h nicads, but it will depend to a large extent on the motor. Some may require, say, a 4½v 1289 flat torch battery or three or four nicads. Float the model in the sink and stow batteries etc, to give correct trim, then cement locating tabs in place, using scrap balsa. Ballast to bring the model to its waterline would best be lead sheet (try a scrapyard) cut with old scissors, laid flat on the hull floor and, when correct, cemented in place. For free running, insert the rudder and carefully bend the wire, holding it close to the tube with, if possible, taper-nose pliers, so that it makes friction contact with a scrap of balsa cemented on the deck as drawn.

Simple though this model is, it does offer an opportunity to try making something and to use imagination and ingenuity to decorate and detail it. If you enjoy building and running it, well, welcome aboard!

Appendix 2 – National Bodies

National or centralised bodies controlling different aspects of modelling include:

AIRCRAFT (all types)
Society of Model Aeronautical Engineers Ltd., Kimberley House, Vaughan Road, Leicester.

CARS
British Radio Car Association, 6 Queensway, Queensbury, Bradford, W. Yorks.
British Slot Car Racing Association, C. Gooding, 47 Salisbury Close, Alton, Hants.

MODEL ENGINEERING (all types)
Northern Federation: Mrs. Moore, New Park Works, The Old Forge, Stapleford, Melton Mowbray, Leics,
Midlands: R. E. G. Humphries, 71 Rosemary Crescent, Woodsetton, Dudley, West Midlands.
Southern Federation: B. Thompson, 35 Rivers Hill, Wootton-at-Stone, Nr. Ware, Herts.

MODEL POWER BOATS (all types)
Model Power Boat Association of Great Britain Ltd., G. Metcalf, 3 Spring View Road, Ware, Herts.

MODEL YACHTS (all types)
Model Yachting Association, R. R. Potts, 8 Sherard Road, Eltham, London SE9 6EP.

MODEL RAILWAYS
There is no single central body, but there are several national associations for specific gauges or scales. A visit to the Public Library is the simplest way to locate clubs in the area, or a local model shop should be able to advise.

Please note that with the exception of the S.M.A.E. all officials work on a voluntary basis and have limited time. They will put you in touch with the nearest club who should be able to resolve queries. Please always include a stamped, self-addressed envelope in any correspondence anticipating a reply.

Appendix 3 – Sources

Magazines published in Britain include:
  AEROMODELLER (monthly)
  RADIO CONTROL MODELS (monthly)
  RADIO MODELLER (monthly)
  MODEL BOATS (monthly)
  SCALE MODELS (monthly)
  MODEL ENGINEER (twice monthly)
  MILITARY MODELLING (monthly)
  MODEL CARS (monthly)
  YOUR MODEL RAILWAY (monthly)
(All the above published by ASP Ltd., Wolsey House, Wolsey Road, Hemel Hempstead, Herts. HP2 4SS)

  RAILWAY MODELLER (monthly)
  MODEL RAILWAY CONSTRUCTOR (monthly)
  AIRFIX MAGAZINE (monthly)
  MODEL SHIPWRIGHT (quarterly)
  MODEL YACHTING NEWS (quarterly, direct, 33 Yorke Gardens, Reigate, Surrey)
  SAM 35 SPEAKS (monthly to SAM 35 members – vintage model aircraft)
  ENGINEERING IN MINIATURE (monthly)

The advertisement columns of periodicals provide guidance to manufacturers and importers of kits, fittings and materials, model shops, mail order suppliers, etc.

Construction plans for models of all types come from one main source: MAP Plans Service, Wolsey House, Wolsey Road, Hemel Hempstead, Herts, HP2 4SS, who publish five separate catalogues of model plans totalling several thousand in all.

Plans Handbook No. 1 – Free flight and control line aircraft.

Plans Handbook No. 2 – Model power boats, yachts, some cars, hovercraft, etc.

Plans Handbook No. 3 – Model Engineering subjects – steam locomotives, traction, petrol, stationary engines, etc.

Plans Handbook No. 4 – Radio-controlled aircraft of all types.

Plans Handbook No. 5 – Scale aircraft, (R/C, F/F, C/L, general drawings, etc.).

Some museums supply scale plans of full-size ships, locomotives, etc., and there are specialist firms supplying such drawings who advertise in the appropriate magazine(s). Most such drawings do not give structural details for model construction, which must therefore be decided by the intending builder. Exceptions are plans for scale radio-controlled aircraft.

Books on various aspects of modelling are reasonably plentiful and most are also advertised from time to time in the appropriate model magazine(s). The largest range by far, covering all the popular branches of modelling, is published by Argus Books Ltd., 1 Golden Square, London W1R 3AB, who will supply a list on receipt of a stamped addressed envelope (230×100 mm or similar).

☆ ☆ ☆ ☆ ☆

Model Magic

Transmission times on Channel Four   See Press for details

Programme 1 **MODELS AND HISTORY**
Sunday July 6, 1986.

Programme 2 **MODEL CARS AND TRAMS**
Sunday July 13, 1986.

Programme 3 **MODEL SHIPS AND YACHTS**
Sunday July 20, 1986.

Programme 4 **MODEL AIRCRAFT**
Sunday July 27, 1986.

Programme 5 **MODEL RAILWAYS**
Sunday August 3, 1986.

Programme 6 **THE MINIATURE ENGINEER**
Sunday August 10, 1986.

INTRODUCED BY BOB SYMES

PRODUCED BY ANDREW CROCKART

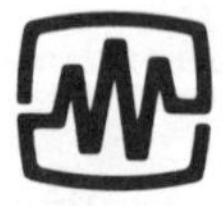 *An Ulster Television Production for Channel Four*

© 1985